THE BUTTER FLAVOR Crisco® COOKBOOK

Since 1911, good cooks have used Crisco® shortening for their baking and frying. Now this famous product has been joined by new Butter Flavor Crisco®. Because it's an all-vegetable shortening, Butter Flavor Crisco gives you the same superior cooking performance you've come to expect from Crisco. And it gives baked and fried foods a rich, buttery taste that consumers preferred 4 to 1 over margarine in a blind taste test.

The recipes in this book demonstrate the versatility of Butter Flavor Crisco. It can be substituted for butter or margarine in all kinds of recipes, from an elegant party cake to a simple grilled cheese sandwich. Try it in our recipes and in favorites of your own. We think you'll agree that Butter Flavor Crisco is the best thing to happen to cooking since Crisco!

© 1983 Procter & Gamble

Design, recipe development, photography and production by Cy DeCosse Incorporated. Minneapolis.
Color separations by The Hennegan Company, Cincinnati.
Printed by Moebius Printing, Milwaukee.

Crisco
BUTTER FLAVOR
FINEST VEGETABLE SHORTENING
ARTIFICIALLY FLAVORED

Introducing Butter Flavor Crisco

What is Butter Flavor Crisco? Like Crisco, Butter Flavor Crisco is made from the finest vegetable oils (soybean and palm) which are partially hydrogenated for freshness and consistency. Artificial buttery flavoring and coloring are added. Butter Flavor Crisco gives you rich, buttery taste with absolutely no cholesterol.

Use Butter Flavor Crisco as an alternative to butter or margarine in your baking and frying. In most recipes, butter or margarine can be replaced by an equal amount of Butter Flavor Crisco. Because Butter Flavor Crisco melts differently, it cannot be substituted for butter or margarine in all candy recipes. The candy recipes in this book were specially formulated to be made with Butter Flavor Crisco. Because it is a shortening, Butter Flavor Crisco is not intended for use as a spread on foods like toast or crackers.

Using Butter Flavor Crisco offers many advantages. Butter Flavor Crisco requires no refrigeration, so it's ready to use without softening. It is easier to blend than butter or margarine. Unlike butter or margarine, Butter Flavor Crisco does not contain water, so it doesn't spatter or scorch at frying temperatures. It gives baked goods a better texture than butter or margarine. Butter Flavor Crisco costs significantly less than butter and gives baked and fried foods more buttery flavor than margarine.

Use Butter Flavor Crisco whenever you want to give baked or fried foods a buttery flavor. It's great for cookies, cakes, pie fillings and other desserts. It gives eggs, fish, hashed browns and other fried foods a buttery flavor. Use it for deep frying appetizers, doughnuts or snacks. Pop popcorn in Butter Flavor Crisco. Try it for moist, tender muffins, pancakes and quick breads. Main dishes, vegetables, yeast breads, sauces and many other foods are good uses for Butter Flavor Crisco.

Butter Flavor Crisco Bakes Better than Butter or Margarine

Layer cake baked with Butter Flavor Crisco is lighter and higher than cake made with margarine.

Identical layer cake baked with margarine is denser and has less volume.

Chocolate chip cookie made with Butter Flavor Crisco is moist and chewy, with higher volume.

Identical cookie recipe made with butter produces a crisper cookie that bakes into a flatter shape.

Butter Flavor Crisco Fries Better than Butter or Margarine

At 365°F, Butter Flavor Crisco cooks fish and other fried foods evenly without burning or splattering.

Butter begins to spatter, scorch and smoke at 300°F or lower, causing fried foods to stick and burn.

Eggs fried in Butter Flavor Crisco cook evenly without discoloration.

Eggs fried in margarine form a tough, brown crust around the edge.

5

Baking Tips

Proper utensils, good ingredients and accurate techniques are the keys to successful baking. To get the best results from the recipes in this book, use the ingredients and pan sizes specified. Ingredients like flour, sugar, Butter Flavor Crisco, eggs, liquid and leavenings (such as baking powder and baking soda) are essential to the product's structure and should not be adjusted or substituted. If you want to be creative, you can vary spices, nuts, chocolate chips and any decoration or garnish.

Measure Butter Flavor Crisco by scooping it from the can with a rubber spatula. Press it firmly into standard nested cups or spoons; level off with a straight edge.

Liquids should be measured in a liquid measuring cup that has a rim and spout. Set it on a level surface and read at eye level.

Flour should be spooned lightly into a nested measuring cup, taking care not to pack it down. Sifting is not necessary. Spoon cup to overflowing, then level across the top with a straight edge. Measure granulated and confectioners' sugar using this same method.

Proper oven temperature is important, since overbaking or underbaking is the most common cause of less-than-perfect results. Remember to preheat your oven to the temperature specified in the recipe for at least 15 minutes before baking. When using glass baking dishes, reduce the oven temperature by 25°. Bake for the amount of time called for in the recipe. If a time range is given, test for doneness after the minimum amount of time.

Insert a wooden pick into the center of cakes and quick breads. If the pick comes out clean, the product is done. When a cake is done, the center will spring back when touched lightly. Tap yeast breads to test for doneness. The loaf will have a hollow sound when done. Most cookies are done when they turn light brown.

Store most baked items in covered containers. Cakes and other desserts that have whipped cream toppings or cream fillings should be stored in the refrigerator. Cakes, breads, rolls and cookies all freeze well. Cakes and cookies freeze best when they are unfrosted. Wrap them tightly and label before freezing. Most baked items should be thawed at room temperature.

Cool cookies, cakes and other baked items on a wire rack. Cookies should be removed from the pan just after baking. Cakes and quick breads should be cooled in the pan for 5 to 10 minutes, then removed from the pan to cool completely. Yeast breads should be removed from the pan immediately and cooled on a wire rack.

Frying Tips

Correct temperatures, proper utensils and a quality shortening like Butter Flavor Crisco are needed for good frying results. There are several types of frying. Generally, *fry* means to cook in fat over direct heat. *Pan-fry* means to cook in a small amount of fat in a slightly preheated pan on a range top. This method works well for smaller cuts of meat or fish.

Pans for successful frying include heavy cast aluminum, enameled cast-iron and those with nonstick surfaces. Pans should be clean and dry before frying. After adding Butter Flavor Crisco, heat the pan to frying temperature. Most recipes in this book direct you to fry or sauté ("cook and stir") over medium heat. For best results, do not add food until Butter Flavor Crisco melts completely.

Sauté means to cook in a small amount of fat in a shallow, open pan on top of the stove. Chopped, minced or diced vegetables and meats are often cooked in this way. Butter Flavor Crisco is excellent for sautéing. Many cookbooks recommend using a combination of butter and oil for sautéing — butter for flavor and oil to prevent smoking and burning. Butter Flavor Crisco provides the frying performance of oil as well as a buttery flavor.

Stir-fry means to fry foods quickly over high heat, stirring and tossing constantly. The key to this frying method is speed, so foods must be thinly sliced or shredded. Chinese cooking often uses this technique.

Amount of Butter Flavor Crisco affects your results. The more you use, the faster the heat will penetrate and the quicker the food will cook. Generally, foods cook best when pan-fried in enough Butter Flavor Crisco to form a layer ⅛ inch deep when melted in the pan. Food to be fried should be dry on the surface. Wet food will not brown properly. Several recipes in this book call for dredging meats in flour to help them brown.

To cook evenly, foods for deep-frying should be of uniform size. Fry only a few at a time. Overcrowding food lowers the temperature of the fat. Remove food with a slotted spoon and drain on paper towels. Between batches, remove any food particles from the fat. After frying, allow Butter Flavor Crisco to cool slightly. Strain through several layers of cheesecloth into the container, cover and refrigerate. Butter Flavor Crisco can be reused once or twice for deep-frying.

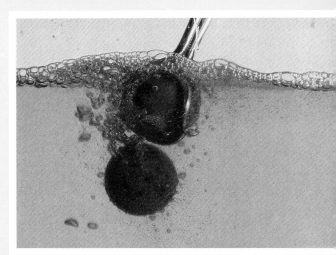

Deep-fat frying means to cook food by completely immersing it in hot fat. Butter and margarine are unsuitable for deep-frying because of their low smoking points. Butter Flavor Crisco gives you good deep-frying results with a buttery flavor.

Equipment for deep-frying includes a deep-fat fryer or deep, heavy saucepan. You should also have a long-handled tongs for turning foods and a slotted metal spoon for removing them.

Heat Butter Flavor Crisco to the depth and temperature called for in the recipe. Use a deep-fat frying thermometer to test the temperature. Be sure to place the bulb so it doesn't touch the bottom of the pan. Constant temperature is important. If the temperature is too low, the food will absorb the fat. If it is too high, the exterior of the food will be overdone and the interior underdone.

Menu Suggestions

Butter Flavor Crisco makes it easy and economical to make all kinds of tasty dishes, from soups to desserts. Pictured here are some ideas for combining the recipes in this book into attractive and nutritious meals. When planning your own menus, keep in mind the following considerations.

Nutrition. The Basic Four Food Groups are a good guide for planning daily meals. A balanced adult diet should include these foods every day:

Meat Group (including seafood, eggs, poultry and other protein-rich foods) — 2 servings

Fruits and Vegetables Group — 4 servings

Breads and Cereals Group (including pasta, rice and starchy vegetables) — 4 servings

Milk Group (including other dairy products) — 2 servings (3 to 4 for children)

Butter Flavor Crisco helps you cook nutritious meals because it adds no cholesterol to foods.

Color, Texture and Flavor. Meals are more enjoyable if they feature a variety of colors, textures and flavors. If your main dish is rather colorless, choose a colorful vegetable or salad. Crunchy vegetables or chewy hard rolls can help add texture to an otherwise soft menu. Make sure your meal combines a variety of flavors. For example, if your main dish contains cheese, you would not want to serve a vegetable with cheese sauce.

Season and Budget. Plan menus that are appropriate to the season of the year. Chilled soups and main dish salads are best for summer meals. Hearty stews and warm desserts make good eating in chilly weather. You'll get better quality and save money if you buy fresh fruits and vegetables when they are in season. Buying in quantity is another good way to economize. Proper cooking and imaginative seasoning can make inexpensive foods into gourmet fare.

Main Dish	Accompaniment (choose one)	Dessert (choose one)
Basted Roast Turkey, p. 51	Fresh Green Vegetable (Broccoli, Peas or Carrots) Sweet Potato Dressing, p. 89	Applesauce Pie, p. 146 Cranberry Orange Cake, p. 118 Pumpkin Cake With Spice Topping, p. 123
Beef Burgundy, p. 36	Tossed Green Salad	Crêpes With Orange Sauce, p. 147
Beef Ragout, p. 37	Fresh Green Vegetable (Broccoli, Peas or Carrots)	Applesauce Pie, p. 146 Easy Fruit Cobbler, p. 147
Beef Stew, p. 37	Baked Potato Wedges, p. 86 Bakery Rolls or Bread Sticks	Easy Fruit Cobbler, p. 147 Zucchini Cake, p. 120
Broiled Fish Fillets, p. 56	Green Beans Amandine, p. 78 Italian Rice & Vegetables, p. 80 Spinach Puff, p. 84	Chocolate-Chocolate Chip Cake, p. 119
Cheese-Stuffed Chicken Breasts, p. 47	Fettuccini With Mushrooms, p. 88 Summer Vegetable Sauté, p. 77	Chocolate Mint Parfait Squares, p. 151
Chicken and Biscuit Bake, p. 48	Baked Potato Wedges, p. 86 Carrot Patties, p. 82	Chocolate Cream Pie, p. 145 Orange Coconut Bars, p. 142
Chicken, Ham and Broccoli Crêpes, p. 53	Bakery Rolls or Bread Sticks Tossed Green Salad	Layered Fruit Bars, p. 141
Chicken in Wine Sauce, p. 48	Fettuccini With Mushrooms, p. 88 Herbed Brussels Sprouts and Carrots, p. 79	Chocolate Cake, p. 114 Crêpes With Orange Sauce, p. 147
Chicken With Herbed Rice, p. 49	Herbed Brussels Sprouts and Carrots, p. 79 Sweet and Sour Beets, p. 80	Apple Maple Steamed Pudding, p. 150 Butter Pecan Cake, p. 120

Main Dish	Accompaniment (choose one)	Dessert (choose one)
Clam & Vegetable Pot Pie, p. 61	Baked Potato Wedges, p. 86	Toffee Bars, p. 142
Cornish Hens With Fruit Stuffing, p. 52	Sweet and Sour Beets, p. 80	Chocolate Mint Parfait Squares, p. 151
Crab Newburg, p. 60	Carrot Patties, p. 82 Italian Rice & Vegetables, p. 80	Pound Cake, p. 119
Creole Pork Chops, p. 46	Cabbage & Noodles, p. 79 Carrot Patties, p. 82	Butter Pecan Cake, p. 120 Toffee Bars, p. 142
Curried Lamb Stew, p. 44	Fried Eggplant, p. 88	Applesauce Pie, p. 146
Deep-Fried Frog Legs, p. 57	Carrot Patties, p. 82 Herbed Brussels Sprouts and Carrots, p. 79	Chocolate Mint Parfait Squares, p. 151 Peach Refrigerator Squares, p. 151
Fish and Vegetable Broil, p. 56	Hashed Brown Potatoes, p. 87 Twice-Baked Potatoes, p. 86	Chocolate Cream Pie, p. 145 Yellow Cake, p. 114
Flemish Pot Roast, p. 38	Tossed Green Salad	Brownies, p. 140
Italian Meatloaf, p. 40	Green Beans Amandine, p. 78 Italian Rice & Vegetables, p. 80 Twice-Baked Potatoes, p. 86	Chocolate-Chocolate Chip Cake, p. 119 Peach Refrigerator Squares, p. 151
Lamb Meatballs With Herb Tomato Sauce, p. 45	Fried Eggplant, p. 88	Orange Coconut Bars, p. 142 Zucchini Cake, p. 120
Liver & Onions, p. 37	Mexican-Style Corn, p. 81 Rutabaga Au Gratin, p. 87	Banana Cream Pie, p. 146 Peach Refrigerator Squares, p. 151
Mushroom-Filled Meat Loaf, p. 40	Carrot Patties, p. 82 Scalloped Corn, p. 81 Twice-Baked Potatoes, p. 86	Orange Yogurt Cake, p. 127 Rhubarb Cake With Spice Topping, p. 123
Oriental Casserole, p. 41	Bakery Rolls or Bread Sticks Carrot Patties, p. 82	Carrot Cake With Cream Cheese Glaze, p. 124
Oven-Fried Chicken, p. 47	Herbed Brussels Sprouts and Carrots, p. 79	Chocolate-Chocolate Chip Cake, p. 119
Pan Fried Fish Fillets, p. 55	Green Beans Amandine, p. 79 Vegetable-Stuffed Green Peppers, p. 85	Chocolate Cake, p. 114 Yellow Cake, p. 114
Paprika Chicken, p. 50	Herbed Brussels Sprouts and Carrots, p. 79	Almond Shortbread Bars, p. 143 Pound Cake, p. 119
Pepper Steak, p. 35	Bakery Rolls or Bread Sticks Tossed Green Salad	Ice Cream With Topping, p. 154-155 Orange Coconut Bars, p. 142
Reuben Sandwich, p. 42	Baked Potato Wedges, p. 86	Vanilla Cake With Creamy Chocolate Frosting, p. 115
Salmon Croquettes, p. 58	Herbed Brussels Sprouts and Carrots, p. 79	Brownies, p. 140 Yellow Cake, p. 114
Sautéed Scallops, p. 57	Italian Rice & Vegetables, p. 80 Twice-Baked Potatoes, p. 86	Brandy Peach Cake With Brown Sugar Glaze, p. 121
Scalloped Oysters, p. 60	Baked Potato Wedges, p. 86	Applesauce Spice Cake, p. 117
Shrimp and Vegetable Stir-Fry, p. 59	Baked Potato Wedges, p. 86	Fudgy Coconut Bars, p. 143 Pound Cake, p. 119
Stuffed Round Steak, p. 39	Herbed Brussels Sprouts and Carrots, p. 79	Pecan Pie, p. 144
Sweet and Spicy Barbecued Chicken, p. 51	Green Beans Amandine, p. 78 Mexican-Style Corn, p. 81	Coconut Pineapple Upside-Down Cake, p. 122
Turkey A La King, p. 52	Carrot Patties, p. 82	Pumpkin Cake With Spice Topping, p. 123
Veal in Sour Cream Sauce, p. 44	Carrot Patties, p. 82 Fettuccini With Mushrooms, p. 88	Bananas Royale, p. 150

APPETIZERS SOUPS & SNACKS

← Potato Soup

1 pound red potatoes (about 8 small),
    peeled, cut into ½-inch cubes
2 cups water
½ teaspoon salt
¼ cup Butter Flavor Crisco
¾ cup chopped celery
½ cup chopped onions
2 medium carrots, finely chopped
3 tablespoons all-purpose flour
3 cups milk
¾ teaspoon salt
¼ teaspoon white pepper
⅛ teaspoon dried thyme leaves

Place potatoes in 2-quart saucepan. Add water and salt. Heat to boiling. Reduce heat; cover and simmer for 10 to 15 minutes, or until tender. Drain.

In large skillet melt Butter Flavor Crisco. Add celery, onions and carrots. Cook and stir over medium heat until tender. Stir in flour. Add to potatoes in saucepan. Stir in milk, salt, white pepper and thyme. Cook and stir over medium heat until bubbly. Continue to cook and stir for 1 minute, or until thickened. Remove from heat. **4 to 6 servings**

← French Onion Soup

1 extra large onion (1 pound)
3 tablespoons Butter Flavor Crisco
1 clove garlic, minced
1 tablespoon all-purpose flour
5 cups water
¼ cup white wine, optional
3 tablespoons instant beef bouillon
   granules
1 tablespoon instant chicken bouillon
   granules
1 teaspoon Worcestershire sauce
   Seasoned croutons
   Grated Parmesan cheese

Peel onion. Cut in half lengthwise, then crosswise into thin slices.

In 3-quart saucepan melt Butter Flavor Crisco. Add onion and garlic. Cook over medium heat for about 20 minutes, or until onion is soft and transparent, stirring occasionally. Stir in flour. Add water, wine, beef and chicken bouillon granules and Worcestershire sauce. Heat to boiling. Reduce heat; cover and simmer for 15 minutes.

Ladle soup into individual serving bowls. Top with seasoned croutons and sprinkle with Parmesan cheese. **4 to 6 servings**

Cheese Soup

⅓ cup Butter Flavor Crisco
½ cup chopped celery
⅓ cup chopped onion
⅓ cup all-purpose flour
¼ teaspoon salt
⅛ teaspoon black or white pepper
1 can (10½ ounces) chicken broth
2 cups milk
3 cups shredded Colby or Cheddar
   cheese
⅛ teaspoon liquid smoke

In 3-quart saucepan melt Butter Flavor Crisco. Add celery and onion. Cook and stir over medium heat until tender. Stir in flour, salt and pepper. Cook and stir until bubbly. Blend in chicken broth and milk. Cook and stir for 8 to 10 minutes, or until mixture comes to boil and thickens. Remove from heat.

Add cheese, 1 cup at a time, stirring to melt after each addition. Stir in liquid smoke. Garnish each serving with *bacon bits*, if desired. **4 to 6 servings**

Vegetable Beef Soup →

2 tablespoons Butter Flavor Crisco
1 to 1½ pounds beef stew meat, cut
   into ¾-inch pieces
3 cups water
1 can (28 ounces) whole tomatoes,
   undrained, cut up
1 can (10¾ ounces) onion soup
½ teaspoon pepper
½ teaspoon dried marjoram leaves
¼ teaspoon dried thyme leaves
1 bay leaf
1½ cups potato cubes (½-inch cubes)
1 cup sliced carrots
½ cup sliced celery
1 cup frozen whole kernel corn
1 cup frozen green beans

In Dutch oven melt Butter Flavor Crisco. Add stew meat. Cook and stir over medium-high heat until meat is browned. Add water, tomatoes, onion soup, pepper, marjoram, thyme and bay leaf. Heat to boiling. Reduce heat; cover and simmer for 1 hour. Add potatoes, carrots and celery. Cover and simmer for 40 to 50 minutes, or until vegetables are tender, stirring occasionally. Add corn and green beans. Re-cover and simmer for 5 to 10 minutes, or until beans are tender. **6 to 8 servings**

Cream of Spinach Soup

⅓ cup Butter Flavor Crisco
⅓ cup chopped onion
⅓ cup all-purpose flour
1 teaspoon salt
¼ teaspoon pepper
⅛ teaspoon ground nutmeg
4¼ cups milk
1 package (10 ounces) frozen chopped
   spinach, thawed and drained
   thoroughly

In 3-quart saucepan melt Butter Flavor Crisco. Add onion. Cook and stir over medium heat until onion is tender. Stir in flour, salt, pepper and nutmeg. Blend in milk. Cook and stir over medium heat until bubbly. Continue to cook and stir for 1 minute, or until thickened. Stir in spinach. Remove from heat.

Cream of Mushroom Soup: Omit nutmeg and spinach. Add 3 cups sliced fresh mushrooms (8 ounces) to Butter Flavor Crisco and onions. Cook and stir for about 4 minutes, or until mushrooms and onion are tender. Continue as directed.

4 to 6 servings

15

Wild Rice Soup ⭠

½ cup uncooked wild rice
2 cups water
½ teaspoon salt
3 tablespoons Butter Flavor Crisco
½ cup chopped green pepper
½ cup chopped celery
⅓ cup chopped onion
1 clove garlic, minced
2 tablespoons all-purpose flour
1½ teaspoons instant chicken bouillon
    granules
½ teaspoon salt
⅛ teaspoon pepper
⅛ teaspoon bouquet garni seasoning
¾ cup cubed fully cooked ham
1 medium carrot, grated
2 tablespoons snipped fresh parsley
2 cups milk
2 cups half-and-half

In 2-quart saucepan combine wild rice, water and salt. Heat to boiling. Reduce heat; cover and simmer for 30 minutes, or until tender. Drain in colander. Set aside.

In 2-quart saucepan melt Butter Flavor Crisco. Add green pepper, celery, onion and garlic. Cook and stir over medium heat for about 7 minutes, or until tender. Stir in flour, bouillon granules, salt, pepper and bouquet garni. Add cooked rice, ham, carrot, parsley, milk and half-and-half. Cook over medium heat for 15 to 20 minutes, or until very hot, stirring occasionally. **4 to 6 servings**

16

Garden Fish Chowder

2 tablespoons Butter Flavor Crisco
1 medium green pepper, chopped
1 cup thinly sliced celery, cut on diagonal
¼ cup chopped green onion
⅛ teaspoon instant minced garlic
1 can (28 ounces) whole peeled tomatoes, undrained, cut up
2 cups water
1 teaspoon instant chicken bouillon granules
¼ teaspoon salt
¼ teaspoon dried basil leaves
⅛ teaspoon dried dill weed
3 to 4 drops hot red pepper sauce
1 cup frozen whole kernel corn
1 pound fresh white fish fillets, ½ inch thick, cut into 1-inch chunks

In 3-quart saucepan melt Butter Flavor Crisco. Add green pepper, celery, green onion and garlic. Cook and stir over medium heat until tender. Stir in tomatoes, water, bouillon granules, salt, basil, dill weed and red pepper sauce. Heat to boiling. Reduce heat; cover and simmer for 15 minutes to blend flavors.

Stir in corn. Gently stir in fish. Cook over medium heat for about 5 minutes, or until fish flakes easily with fork, stirring gently.   **6 to 8 servings**

Toasted Sesame Seed Wafers

¼ cup sesame seed
1½ cups all-purpose flour
¾ teaspoon salt
⅛ teaspoon paprika
Dash garlic powder
½ cup Butter Flavor Crisco
3 or 4 drops hot red pepper sauce
3 to 4 tablespoons cold water
1 tablespoon milk

Preheat oven to 375°F. Spread sesame seed in 8 × 8 × 2-inch baking pan. Bake for 6 to 10 minutes, or until golden brown. Transfer to small dish; set aside.

In medium mixing bowl combine flour, salt, paprika and garlic powder. Cut in Butter Flavor Crisco to form coarse crumbs. Stir in 3 tablespoons toasted sesame seed. Add red pepper sauce to 4 tablespoons water. Add liquid, 1 tablespoon at a time, mixing with fork until particles are moistened and cling together. Form dough into ball.

Roll dough ⅛ inch thick on lightly floured board. Cut with 2- or 2½-inch cookie cutter. Transfer cutouts to ungreased baking sheet. Brush with milk. Sprinkle lightly with remaining sesame seed. Bake at 375°F for 12 to 15 minutes, or until light golden brown. Cool. Store in covered container.
4 to 4½ dozen wafers

Caramel Corn

½ cup packed brown sugar
⅓ cup light corn syrup
¼ cup Butter Flavor Crisco
½ teaspoon vanilla
2 quarts popped popcorn
1 cup coarsely chopped blanched
  almonds (optional)

Preheat oven to 300°F. Generously grease baking sheet. In Dutch oven blend brown sugar, corn syrup, Butter Flavor Crisco and vanilla. Cook over medium-high heat for about 2 minutes, or until light and foamy, stirring constantly. Remove from heat. Add popcorn, tossing to coat. Stir in almonds. Spread on prepared baking sheet.

Bake at 300°F for 15 minutes, stirring once. Cool. Break into bite-size pieces. Store in covered container.

Coconut Caramel Corn: Follow the recipe above, adding ¾ cup flaked coconut with almonds.

2 quarts caramel corn

↑ Fried Mozzarella Sticks

6 ounces mozzarella or Monterey Jack
  cheese (solid block)
2 tablespoons plus 1 teaspoon
  milk, divided
¼ cup all-purpose flour
1 egg
¾ cup seasoned fine dry bread crumbs
  Butter Flavor Crisco for frying
  Prepared pizza or taco sauce

Cut cheese into 2½-inch sticks. Place 2 tablespoons milk in shallow bowl. Dip sticks in milk; coat with flour. In small bowl beat egg and remaining 1 teaspoon milk together. Dip floured cheese sticks in egg mixture; roll in bread crumbs. Refrigerate for at least 15 minutes.

In deep-fat fryer or deep saucepan heat 2 to 3 inches Butter Flavor Crisco to 375°F. Fry several at a time in hot oil for 45 seconds to 1 minute, or until golden brown and sticks float to top. Drain on paper towels. Serve immediately with pizza sauce.

Mexican Cheese Sticks: Follow the recipe above, substituting 6 ounces Monterey Jack block cheese for the mozzarella cheese. Substitute prepared taco sauce for the pizza sauce.

About 2 dozen appetizers

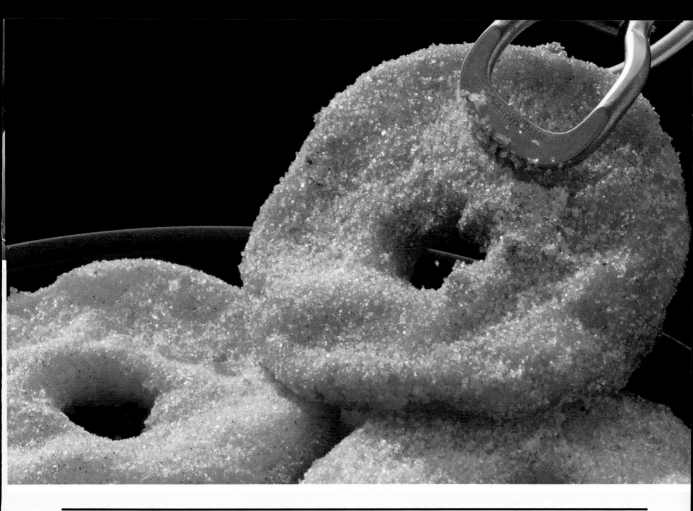

Deep-Fried Apple Rings ↑

1 cup all-purpose flour
2 tablespoons cornstarch
½ cup plus 1 tablespoon sugar, divided
½ teaspoon baking powder
½ teaspoon salt
1 cup milk
1 egg
½ teaspoon cinnamon
3 medium baking apples
  Butter Flavor Crisco for frying

In medium mixing bowl mix flour, cornstarch, 1 tablespoon sugar, baking powder and salt. In small bowl beat together milk and egg. Gradually add to flour mixture, beating with fork until well blended. Refrigerate for 1 hour.

In small bowl combine remaining ½ cup sugar and cinnamon. Set aside. Peel and core apples. Cut crosswise into rings, ¼-inch thick.

In deep-fat fryer or deep saucepan heat 1½ to 2 inches Butter Flavor Crisco to 375°F. Dip apple slices in batter, allowing excess to drip back into bowl. Fry a few at a time in hot oil for 3 to 5 minutes, or until golden brown, turning frequently. Drain on paper towels. Dredge in cinnamon-sugar mixture. Serve immediately or keep warm in 175°F oven.   **About 3½ dozen rings**

19

Seasoned Snack Mix ↕

⅔ cup Butter Flavor Crisco
¾ cup grated Parmesan cheese
2 teaspoons Worcestershire sauce
1 teaspoon Italian seasoning
½ teaspoon garlic salt
⅛ teaspoon onion powder
⅛ teaspoon cayenne
3 cups bite-size rice squares cereal
2 cups round toasted oat cereal
2 cups oyster crackers
2 cups pretzel sticks
1 can (7 ounces) Spanish peanuts

Preheat oven to 325°F. In Dutch oven melt Butter
Flavor Crisco. Remove from heat. Stir in Parmesan
cheese, Worcestershire sauce, Italian seasoning,
garlic salt, onion powder and cayenne. Add rice
squares and toasted oat cereal, oyster crackers,
pretzel sticks and peanuts. Toss to coat. Spread on
12×17½×1-inch jelly roll pan.

Bake at 325°F for 15 to 18 minutes, or until toasted
and golden brown, stirring once after 10 minutes.
Cool. Store in covered container.   **About 10 cups**

Cheesy Onion Wafers

1 tablespoon instant minced onion
1 tablespoon water
1½ cups all-purpose flour
½ teaspoon salt
Dash cayenne
1 cup grated Cheddar cheese
¼ cup grated Parmesan cheese
½ cup Butter Flavor Crisco
3 to 4 tablespoons cold water

Preheat oven to 375°F. In small dish combine onion
and water. Set aside for 5 minutes.

In medium mixing bowl combine flour, salt,
cayenne, Cheddar and Parmesan cheese. Cut in
Butter Flavor Crisco to form coarse crumbs. Stir in
onion mixture. Add water, 1 tablespoon at a time,
mixing with fork until particles are moistened and
cling together. Form dough into ball.

Roll dough ⅛ inch thick on lightly floured board.
Cut shapes with 2- or 2½-inch square cookie cutter.
Transfer cutouts to ungreased baking sheet. Bake at
375°F for 12 to 15 minutes, or until light golden
brown. Cool. Store in covered container.

4½ to 5 dozen wafers

Sausage Roll-Ups

Filling:
¼ pound ground seasoned sausage, crumbled
½ cup chopped mushrooms
3 tablespoons chopped onion
2 tablespoons finely chopped celery
1 tablespoon chopped stuffed green olives
2 teaspoons all-purpose flour

Dough:
1 cup all-purpose flour
1 teaspoon baking powder
1 teaspoon dried parsley flakes
¼ teaspoon salt
¼ cup Butter Flavor Crisco
¼ cup milk

Topping:
2 tablespoons Butter Flavor Crisco, melted
Paprika

For filling, in small skillet combine sausage, mushrooms, onion, celery and olives. Cook and stir over medium-high heat until sausage is no longer pink. Stir in flour. Remove from heat. Set aside.

Preheat oven to 350°F. Lightly grease baking sheet. Set aside.

For dough, in medium mixing bowl combine flour, baking powder, parsley flakes and salt. Cut in Butter Flavor Crisco to form coarse crumbs. Add milk, mixing with fork until particles are moistened and cling together. Form dough into ball. On floured board, knead 8 to 10 times. Continue as directed below. **2½ to 3 dozen appetizers**

How to Assemble Sausage Roll-Ups

Roll dough into a 16 × 6-inch rectangle. Spread filling on dough. Starting with longer side, roll up tightly. Seal seam.

Cut into ½-inch slices. Place on baking sheet. Brush with melted Butter Flavor Crisco.

Sprinkle lightly with paprika. Bake at 350°F for 15 to 18 minutes, or until firm.

Ham and Sauerkraut Balls ✝

2 tablespoons Butter Flavor Crisco
¼ cup finely chopped onion
⅓ cup plus 3 tablespoons all-purpose
   flour, divided
   Dash garlic powder
   Dash cayenne
2 cans (6¾ ounces each) chunk ham,
   drained and flaked
1 can (8 ounces) sauerkraut, rinsed
   and drained
½ cup grated Swiss cheese
1 egg, slightly beaten
2 tablespoons snipped fresh parsley
   Butter Flavor Crisco for frying

In small skillet melt Butter Flavor Crisco. Add onion. Cook and stir over medium heat until tender. Stir in 3 tablespoons flour, garlic powder and cayenne. Cook until mixture thickens, stirring constantly. Transfer mixture to medium mixing bowl. Add ham, sauerkraut, cheese, egg and parsley. Mix thoroughly. Refrigerate for at least 30 minutes.

In deep-fat fryer or deep saucepan heat 2 to 3 inches Butter Flavor Crisco to 375°F. Shape ham mixture by rounded tablespoonfuls into balls. Roll in remaining ⅓ cup flour to coat. Fry a few at a time in hot oil for 2 to 2½ minutes, or until golden brown. Drain on paper towels. Serve immediately or keep warm in 175°F oven. Serve with *Hot Mustard Sauce*, page 28, if desired.

TIP: To make a day ahead, prepare and fry as directed. Cool. Cover and refrigerate. Reheat in single layer on baking sheet at 425°F for 8 to 10 minutes, or until hot.

Corned Beef and Sauerkraut Balls: Follow the recipe above, substituting 1 can (12 ounces) corned beef for the 2 cans chunk ham.

2½ to 3 dozen appetizers

Swedish Cocktail Meatballs →

½ pound lean ground beef
½ pound ground seasoned sausage
½ cup fine dry bread crumbs
(unseasoned)
1 egg
½ teaspoon salt, divided
⅛ teaspoon pepper
⅛ teaspoon ground nutmeg
2 tablespoons Butter Flavor Crisco,
divided
¼ cup finely chopped onion
¼ cup finely chopped celery
2 tablespoons all-purpose flour
1 cup milk
2 tablespoons snipped fresh parsley
Dash ground nutmeg
½ cup dairy sour cream

In large mixing bowl combine beef, sausage, bread crumbs, egg, ¼ teaspoon salt, pepper and ⅛ teaspoon nutmeg. Mix thoroughly. Set aside.

In large skillet melt 1 tablespoon Butter Flavor Crisco. Add onion and celery. Cook and stir over medium heat until tender. Stir into meat mixture.

Shape by rounded teaspoonfuls into balls. In large skillet melt remaining 1 tablespoon Butter Flavor Crisco. Add meatballs; cook over medium heat until firm and golden brown. Remove and drain on paper towels.

Stir flour into drippings in skillet. Blend in milk, parsley, remaining ¼ teaspoon salt and dash nutmeg. Cook and stir over medium heat until mixture thickens. Remove from heat. Blend in sour cream. Add meatballs, stirring to coat. Cook until heated through. Serve with cocktail picks.

About 3 dozen appetizers

Hot Pastry Appetizers ➔

Pastry:
1⅔ cups all-purpose flour
¼ cup grated Parmesan cheese
½ teaspoon salt
⅔ cup Butter Flavor Crisco
3 to 4 tablespoons milk

Filling Variations:

Mushroom:
3 tablespoons Butter Flavor Crisco
8 ounces fresh mushrooms, finely
  chopped (about 2½ cups)
⅓ cup chopped onion
¼ cup snipped fresh parsley
2 tablespoons all-purpose flour
¼ teaspoon garlic powder
¼ teaspoon salt
⅛ teaspoon pepper

Crab:
1 tablespoon Butter Flavor Crisco
¼ cup chopped green onion
¼ cup finely chopped celery
1 package (3 ounces) cream cheese,
  softened
½ cup grated Swiss or Cheddar cheese
1 can (6½ ounces) crab meat, rinsed
  and drained

Ham:
1 tablespoon Butter Flavor Crisco
¼ cup chopped green onion
¼ cup finely chopped celery
3 ounces cream cheese, softened
½ cup grated Cheddar cheese
1 can (6¾ ounces) chunk ham,
  drained and flaked

In medium bowl combine flour, Parmesan cheese and salt. Cut in Butter Flavor Crisco to form coarse crumbs. Add in milk, 1 tablespoon at a time, mixing with fork until particles are moistened and cling together. Form dough into ball. Refrigerate while preparing desired filling.

For mushroom filling, in small skillet melt Butter Flavor Crisco. Add mushrooms, onion and parsley. Cook and stir over medium heat until tender. Add flour, garlic powder, salt and pepper. Continue to cook and stir for 1 minute. Remove from heat.

For crab filling, in small skillet melt Butter Flavor Crisco. Add onion and celery. Cook and stir over medium heat until tender. Remove from heat and set aside. In medium bowl mix cream cheese, Swiss cheese and crab meat. Stir in onion and celery.

For ham filling, in small skillet melt Butter Flavor Crisco. Add onion and celery. Cook and stir over medium heat until tender. Remove from heat and set aside. In medium bowl mix cream cheese, Cheddar cheese and ham. Stir in onion and celery.

Preheat oven to 400°F. To prepare pastry, divide dough in half. Roll each half ⅛ inch thick on lightly floured board. Cut shapes with 2-inch round cookie cutter. Assemble according to directions at right.

Bake at 400°F for 10 to 15 minutes, or until light golden brown. Cool slightly on wire rack. Serve warm. Serve with *dairy sour cream* for dipping, if desired.

TIP: Appetizers may be assembled and refrigerated overnight before baking. Bake at 400°F for 15 to 20 minutes, or until light golden brown.

About 2 dozen appetizers

How to Assemble Hot Pastry Appetizers

To assemble, place 1 cutout on ungreased baking sheet. Place 1 teaspoon filling in center of cutout.

Moisten edges with water. Place another cutout on top.

Press edges together with tines of fork. Repeat for remaining appetizers.

⟵ Deep-Fried Stuffed Mushrooms

  8 ounces whole fresh mushrooms
  1 tablespoon Butter Flavor Crisco
  1 teaspoon grated onion
  1 teaspoon dried parsley flakes
  ½ teaspoon freeze-dried chives
  ½ teaspoon Worcestershire sauce
  ¼ teaspoon salt
     Dash pepper
  ½ cup plus 2 tablespoons fine dry bread
     crumbs (unseasoned), divided
     Butter Flavor Crisco for frying
  1 egg
  1 teaspoon milk

Wash mushrooms and trim stems slightly. Remove stems from mushrooms; set caps aside. Finely chop stems.

In small saucepan combine chopped stems, 1 tablespoon Butter Flavor Crisco, onion, parsley flakes, chives, Worcestershire sauce, salt and pepper. Cook and stir over medium heat until mushrooms are tender. Remove from heat. Stir in 2 tablespoons bread crumbs. Fill caps with stuffing mixture, packing firmly and mounding mixture slightly.

In deep-fat fryer or deep saucepan heat 2 to 3 inches Butter Flavor Crisco to 375°F.

In small bowl beat egg and milk together. Dip filled mushrooms in egg mixture. Roll in remaining ½ cup bread crumbs to coat.

Fry a few at a time in hot oil for 1 to 3 minutes, or until golden brown, turning once. Drain on paper towels. Serve immediately or keep warm in 175.°F oven.

TIP: To make a day ahead, prepare as directed. Coat with egg mixture and crumbs; place on plate. Cover with plastic wrap and refrigerate. Fry as directed, adding 1 to 2 minutes cooking time.

4 to 6 servings

Deep-Fried Zucchini ↟

1½ cups all-purpose flour, divided
2 tablespoons cornstarch
¾ teaspoon lemon pepper
½ teaspoon baking powder
½ teaspoon salt
¼ teaspoon onion powder
1 cup milk
1 egg
1 pound fresh zucchini (about 3 medium)
   Butter Flavor Crisco for frying
   Grated Parmesan cheese

In medium mixing bowl combine 1 cup flour, cornstarch, baking powder, salt, lemon pepper, onion powder, milk and egg. Blend until smooth. Refrigerate for at least 30 minutes.

Cut zucchini into ¼-inch diagonal slices. Rinse and pat dry. Shake slices in remaining ½ cup flour to coat.

In deep-fat fryer or deep saucepan heat 2 to 3 inches Butter Flavor Crisco to 375°F. Dip floured zucchini in chilled batter. Let excess drip back into bowl. Fry a few at a time in hot oil for 4 to 4½ minutes, or until golden brown, turning several times. Drain on paper towels. Serve immediately or keep warm in 175°F oven. Sprinkle with Parmesan cheese before serving.

TIP: To make a day ahead, prepare and fry as directed. Cool. Cover and refrigerate. Reheat in single layer on baking sheet in 425°F oven for about 10 minutes, or until hot. Sprinkle with Parmesan cheese. **4 to 5 dozen appetizers**

Miniature Monte Cristos ➔

6 slices soft white bread, trimmed
  Mustard
6 very thin slices fully cooked ham
6 very thin slices fully cooked turkey
1½ cups shredded Swiss cheese
  Batter:
1 cup buttermilk baking mix
2 eggs
1 can (5⅓ ounces) evaporated milk
¼ teaspoon salt
⅛ teaspoon ground cinnamon
  Butter Flavor Crisco for frying

Prepare as directed under photos below.

TIP: To make a day ahead, prepare and fry as directed. Cool. Cover and refrigerate. Reheat in single layer on baking sheet in 425°F oven for 8 to 10 minutes.   **2 dozen appetizers**

Hot Mustard Sauce

1 tablespoon Butter Flavor Crisco
1 tablespoon all-purpose flour
1 tablespoon dry mustard
¼ teaspoon salt
  Dash pepper
½ cup milk
2 teaspoons prepared mustard
1 teaspoon vinegar

In small saucepan melt Butter Flavor Crisco. Remove from heat. Stir in flour, dry mustard, salt and pepper. Blend in milk. Cook over medium heat until mixture thickens, stirring constantly. Blend in prepared mustard and vinegar. Serve warm or cold.
    ½ cup sauce

How to Prepare Miniature Monte Cristos

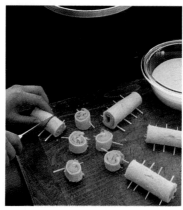

Flatten each slice of trimmed bread with rolling pin. Spread slices with mustard. Top each with one slice ham and one slice turkey. Sprinkle with ¼ cup shredded cheese to within ½ inch of shorter edge. Starting with opposite edge, roll tightly and secure with 4 equally-spaced wooden picks.

For batter, in medium bowl beat together baking mix and eggs. Blend in evaporated milk, salt and cinnamon. In deep-fat fryer or deep saucepan heat 1½ inches Butter Flavor Crisco to 375°F. With serrated knife slice each roll into 4 pieces (each secured with wooden pick).

Dip each piece in batter, allowing some batter to be absorbed. Fry a few at a time in hot oil for 1 to 2 minutes, or until deep golden brown, turning frequently. Drain on paper towels. Serve immediately or keep warm in 175°F oven. Serve with *Hot Mustard Sauce, above,* if desired.

Appetizer Quiche Squares ↑

Pastry:
1¼ cups all-purpose flour
½ teaspoon salt
½ cup Butter Flavor Crisco
2 to 3 tablespoons water

Filling:
3 eggs, slightly beaten
1 can (13 ounces) evaporated milk
2 tablespoons all-purpose flour
½ teaspoon Worcestershire sauce
¼ teaspoon salt
⅛ teaspoon garlic powder
1 can (6¼ ounces) tiny shrimp, drained
1 cup grated Cheddar cheese
½ cup grated carrot
¼ cup chopped onion

Preheat oven to 325°F. In medium bowl combine flour and salt. Cut in Butter Flavor Crisco to form coarse crumbs. Add water, 1 tablespoon at a time, mixing with fork until particles are moistened and cling together. Form dough into ball. Roll into a 10-inch square on lightly floured board. Ease dough into 9 × 2-inch pan. Press excess up around edges of pan to form 1-inch rim. Bake at 325°F for 10 minutes. Set aside.

For filling, in large bowl blend eggs, evaporated milk, flour, Worcestershire sauce, salt and garlic powder. Stir in shrimp, cheese, carrot and onion. Pour into partially-baked pastry. Bake at 325°F for 30 to 35 minutes, or until knife inserted in center comes out clean. Cut into 20 squares.

20 appetizers

Olive Cheese Puffs ↑

1 bottle (5 ounces) stuffed green olives
¾ cup all-purpose flour
⅛ teaspoon dry mustard or cayenne
¼ cup plus 2 tablespoons
    Butter Flavor Crisco
1½ cups shredded sharp Cheddar cheese
1 tablespoon milk
1 teaspoon Worcestershire sauce

Drain olives. Pat dry. Set aside.

In medium bowl combine flour and dry mustard. Cut in Butter Flavor Crisco to form coarse crumbs. Add cheese, tossing to combine. In small bowl or custard cup combine milk and Worcestershire sauce. Add to flour mixture, mixing with fork until particles are moistened and cling together. Form dough into ball. Shape 1 rounded teaspoonful dough around each olive. Place on baking sheet. Refrigerate for at least 30 minutes.

Preheat oven to 400°F. Bake for 10 to 15 minutes, or until light golden brown. Cool slightly on wire rack. Serve warm.   **About 3 dozen appetizers**

Tempura Onion Strings

pictured on page 13

1 large onion (¾ pound)
  Packaged tempura batter mix
  Butter Flavor Crisco for frying
  Salt

Slice onion in half lengthwise, then crosswise into ¼-inch slices. Prepare enough tempura mix according to package directions to yield about 1½ cups. Refrigerate for at least 30 minutes.

In deep-fat fryer or deep saucepan heat 2 to 3 inches Butter Flavor Crisco to 375°F. Dip onion pieces in tempura batter, letting excess drip back into bowl. Fry a few at a time in hot oil for 2 to 3 minutes, or until golden brown, turning two or three times. Drain on paper towels. Sprinkle with salt. Serve immediately or keep warm in 175°F oven.
4 to 6 servings

Deep-Fried Potato Nuggets →

2 medium white potatoes (about 1 pound), peeled, cut into eight pieces
4 slices bacon, cut up
¼ cup finely chopped onion
1 cup thick White Sauce
⅔ cup grated Cheddar cheese
Butter Flavor Crisco for frying
2 eggs
2 tablespoons milk
½ cup all-purpose flour
1½ cups fine dry bread crumbs (unseasoned)

In medium saucepan cover potatoes with water. Heat to boiling. Reduce heat; cover and simmer for about 30 minutes, or until tender.

In small frying pan fry bacon until crisp. Remove with slotted spoon, leaving bacon drippings in pan. Drain bacon on paper towels. Crumble.

In bacon drippings cook and stir onion over medium heat until tender. Drain and discard drippings.

Prepare Thick White Sauce as directed, page 74. In large mixing bowl combine potatoes, onion, crumbled bacon and White Sauce. Blend at low speed of electric mixer until smooth. Stir in cheese.

In deep-fat fryer or deep saucepan heat 2 to 3 inches Butter Flavor Crisco to 375°F.

In small bowl beat eggs and milk together. Place flour in second small bowl. Drop potato mixture by rounded teaspoonfuls into flour. Shape into balls. Dip each ball in egg mixture. Roll in bread crumbs to coat.

Fry a few at a time in hot oil for 1 to 2 minutes, or until golden brown, turning once. Drain on paper towels. Serve immediately or keep warm in 175°F oven.

TIP: To make ahead, prepare and fry as directed. Cool. Cover and refrigerate. Reheat in single layer on baking sheet in 425°F oven for 8 to 10 minutes, or until hot. **3 to 3½ dozen appetizers**

Cream Puff Appetizers →

½ cup water
¼ cup Butter Flavor Crisco
½ cup all-purpose flour
⅛ teaspoon salt
2 eggs

Filling Variations:

Shrimp:
1 package (3 ounces) cream cheese,
   softened
⅓ cup dairy sour cream
2 teaspoons catsup
¼ teaspoon dried tarragon leaves
⅛ teaspoon pepper
   Dash garlic powder
2 cans (6¼ ounces each) tiny shrimp,
   rinsed, drained and chopped
1 can (8 ounces) water chestnuts,
   drained and finely chopped

Chicken:
2 cups finely chopped cooked chicken
⅔ cup mayonnaise or salad dressing
½ cup finely chopped celery
⅓ cup finely chopped almonds
1 hard cooked egg, finely chopped
1½ teaspoons lemon juice
¾ teaspoon salt
¼ teaspoon pepper

Preheat oven to 400°F. In medium saucepan combine water and Butter Flavor Crisco. Heat to rolling boil. Add flour and salt, stirring until mixture forms a ball. Continue to cook and stir for 1 minute. Remove from heat. Add eggs all at once, beating until smooth.

Drop by ½-teaspoonfuls at least 1½ inches apart onto ungreased baking sheet. Bake at 400°F for 20 to 30 minutes, or until golden brown. Cool away from draft. Meanwhile, prepare one of the fillings.

For shrimp filling, in medium mixing bowl blend cream cheese and sour cream. Stir in catsup, tarragon, pepper and garlic powder. Add shrimp and water chestnuts. Mix thoroughly. Cover and refrigerate for at least 30 minutes.

For chicken filling, in medium mixing bowl combine all ingredients. Mix thoroughly. Cover and refrigerate for at least 30 minutes.

To fill, cut off tops of cooled cream puffs. Remove dough filaments from inside. Fill with desired filling. Replace tops.   **About 2 dozen appetizers**

Sautéed Shrimp

2 tablespoons Butter Flavor Crisco
1 large clove garlic, cut into 4 pieces
½ teaspoon dried dill weed
½ pound small fresh shrimp, peeled
   and deveined

In small skillet melt Butter Flavor Crisco. Add garlic and dill weed. Cook and stir over low heat until garlic begins to turn light brown. Discard garlic.

Add shrimp. Cook and stir over medium heat for about 5 minutes, or until shrimp is opaque. Drain on paper towels. Serve immediately with cocktail picks.   **4 to 6 servings**

Caraway Crackers

pictured on page 12

½ cup whole wheat flour
½ cup rye flour
½ cup all-purpose flour
2 tablespoons packed brown sugar
1½ teaspoons whole caraway seed
1 teaspoon baking powder
½ teaspoon baking soda
¼ teaspoon salt
¼ cup Butter Flavor Crisco
½ cup milk
Salt

Preheat oven to 300°F. Lightly grease baking sheets. Set aside.

In medium mixing bowl combine wheat, rye and all-purpose flour, brown sugar, caraway seed, baking powder, baking soda and ¼ teaspoon salt. Cut in Butter Flavor Crisco to form coarse crumbs. Add milk, mixing with fork until particles are moistened and cling together. Form dough into ball.

On floured board, lightly knead for about 3 minutes, or until smooth. Roll dough ⅛ to ¹⁄₁₆ inch thick. Cut shapes with 2-inch round cookie cutter. Place on baking sheet. Prick each cracker with fork 1 or 2 times. Sprinkle tops with salt.

Bake at 300°F for 25 to 30 minutes, or until deep golden brown and firm to the touch. Remove to cooling rack. Cool completely. Store in covered container. **3½ to 4 dozen crackers**

33

Meats & Poultry

→ Pepper Steak

    1- to 1½-pound beef boneless sirloin
      steak
¼ cup Butter Flavor Crisco
 1 clove garlic, cut into 4 pieces
 2 medium green peppers, cut into 1-inch
      pieces
 1 medium onion, thinly sliced and
      separated into rings
 1 can (8 ounces) bamboo shoots, drained
¼ teaspoon salt
¼ teaspoon pepper
⅛ teaspoon ground ginger
 1 teaspoon instant beef bouillon granules
 1 cup hot water
 2 tablespoons soy sauce
 2 tablespoons cornstarch
    Hot cooked rice

Cut steak diagonally across grain into very thin
slices. Cut into strips about 2 inches long. Set aside.

In large skillet melt Butter Flavor Crisco. Add garlic.
Cook over medium heat until garlic turns light
brown. Remove and discard. Add green pepper
and onion. Cook and stir over medium heat until
tender. Add beef strips. Cook until browned. Add
bamboo shoots, salt, pepper and ginger. Dissolve
bouillon granules in hot water. Slowly add to
mixture in skillet. Blend soy sauce and cornstarch
together. Stir into mixture. Heat to boiling. Cook
and stir constantly until mixture thickens. Serve over
rice.   **4 to 6 servings**

Beef Burgundy ↑

3 tablespoons Butter Flavor Crisco
1 medium onion, cut into wedges
2 medium carrots, cut into julienne strips
　 (2 × ¼-inch)
½ cup all-purpose flour
1 teaspoon salt
⅛ teaspoon pepper
　 1½-pounds beef sirloin, cut into 1½-inch
　 cubes
1 can (10¾ ounces) beef broth
1 cup burgundy wine or water
1 cup water
¾ teaspoon dried bouquet garni
1 teaspoon dried parsley flakes
⅛ teaspoon garlic powder
8 ounces fresh mushrooms, sliced
　 Hot cooked rice or egg noodles

In Dutch oven melt Butter Flavor Crisco. Add onion and carrots. Cook and stir over medium heat until tender. Remove from heat.

In large plastic food storage bag combine flour, salt and pepper. Add beef. Shake to coat. Add coated beef and any remaining flour mixture to vegetables. Cook over medium-high heat until beef is browned. Stir in broth, wine, water, bouquet garni, parsley flakes and garlic powder. Heat to boiling. Reduce heat. Stir in mushrooms. Simmer for 10 to 20 minutes, or until mixture thickens and mushrooms are tender, stirring occasionally. Serve over rice or egg noodles. **4 to 6 servings**

Beef Ragout

3 tablespoons Butter Flavor Crisco
1 cup thinly sliced celery
½ cup chopped onion
  1½- to 2-pound beef boneless round
    steak, cut into 1-inch pieces
2 cans (16 ounces each) whole tomatoes,
    undrained and cut up
1 can (6 ounces) tomato paste
1 tablespoon red wine vinegar
1 tablespoon packed brown sugar
2 teaspoons dried parsley flakes
1 teaspoon paprika
½ teaspoon dried oregano leaves
½ teaspoon garlic salt
¼ teaspoon caraway seed
⅛ teaspoon cayenne
1 bay leaf, optional
  Hot cooked rice or egg noodles

In Dutch oven melt Butter Flavor Crisco. Add
celery and onion. Cook and stir over medium heat
until tender. Add beef. Brown over medium-high
heat. Stir in tomatoes, tomato paste, wine vinegar,
brown sugar, parsley flakes, paprika, oregano, garlic
salt, caraway seed, cayenne and bay leaf. Heat to
boiling. Reduce heat. Cover and simmer for 2 to
2½ hours, or until beef is tender, stirring
occasionally. Remove bay leaf. Serve over rice or
egg noodles.   **4 to 6 servings**

Beef Stew

½ cup all-purpose flour
2 teaspoons salt
¼ teaspoon pepper
1½ to 2 pounds beef stew meat, cut into
    1-inch cubes
¼ cup Butter Flavor Crisco
1 small onion, cut into thin wedges
2 cloves garlic, minced
4 medium potatoes, cut into 1-inch cubes
2 stalks celery, cut into ½-inch pieces
2 medium carrots, cut into 1-inch pieces
5 cups water
2 teaspoons dried parsley flakes
¼ cup red wine, optional
1 teaspoon bouquet sauce, optional

In large plastic food storage bag combine flour, salt
and pepper. Add beef. Shake to coat. In Dutch
oven melt Butter Flavor Crisco. Add onion, garlic,
coated beef and any remaining flour mixture. Cook
over medium-high heat until beef is browned. Add
potatoes, celery, carrots, water and parsley flakes.
Heat to boiling. Reduce heat. Cover and simmer for
1½ to 2 hours, or until beef is tender. Add wine
and bouquet sauce during last 30 minutes of
cooking time.   **4 to 6 servings**

Liver and Onions

¼ cup Butter Flavor Crisco
2 medium onions, thinly sliced and
    separated into rings
⅓ cup all-purpose flour
1 teaspoon salt
¼ teaspoon pepper
⅛ teaspoon paprika
  Dash garlic powder
1 pound beef liver, sliced ½ to ¾ inch
    thick, membrane removed

In large skillet melt Butter Flavor Crisco. Add onion.
Cook and stir over medium heat until tender.
Remove from heat.

In large plastic food storage bag combine flour, salt,
pepper, paprika and garlic powder. Add liver.
Shake to coat. Add coated liver to skillet with
onions. Cook over medium heat for 3 to 5 minutes
on each side, or until browned. To serve, arrange
onions over liver.   **4 to 6 servings**

Flemish Pot Roast ↑

2 tablespoons Butter Flavor Crisco
    2½- to 3-pound beef chuck roast
1 cup beer, or 1 cup water plus 2 tea-
    spoons instant beef bouillon granules
¾ teaspoon garlic salt
¼ teaspoon pepper
4 whole allspice
1 large bay leaf
4 small white potatoes, quartered
3 medium carrots, peeled and cut into
    3-inch pieces
1 medium onion, cut into wedges
Gravy:
¼ cup all-purpose flour
¼ cup cold water
½ teaspoon bouquet sauce, optional

Preheat oven to 325°F. In large skillet melt Butter Flavor Crisco. Add beef. Brown over medium-high heat. Transfer beef and drippings to roasting pan or 3-quart casserole. Add beer, garlic salt, pepper, allspice and bay leaves. Cover. Bake at 325°F for 1½ hours. Arrange potatoes, carrots and onion around beef. Re-cover and bake for 1 to 1½ hours longer, or until meat is fork tender. Remove bay leaf. Transfer beef and vegetables to platter. Cover with foil and set aside.

For gravy, pour drippings into 2-cup measure. Add enough water to make 2 cups. Pour into 1-quart saucepan. Blend flour and ¼ cup cold water together. Blend into juices. Heat to boiling, stirring constantly. Cook and stir until mixture thickens. Stir in bouquet sauce. Serve with pot roast.

4 to 6 servings

Stuffed Round Steak →

 5 tablespoons Butter Flavor Crisco, divided
¼ cup finely chopped onion
¼ cup finely chopped celery
1½ cups fine dry bread crumbs
½ teaspoon salt
¼ teaspoon pepper
¼ teaspoon ground sage
¼ teaspoon dried thyme leaves
⅛ teaspoon garlic powder
 1 teaspoon instant beef bouillon granules
½ cup hot water
    1½- to 2-pound beef boneless round steak, ½ inch thick, pounded to ¼-inch thickness
 1 can (10½ ounces) onion soup
½ cup water

Preheat oven to 350°F. In small skillet melt 3 tablespoons Butter Flavor Crisco. Add onion and celery. Cook and stir over medium heat until tender. Transfer to medium mixing bowl. Add bread crumbs, salt, pepper, sage, thyme and garlic powder. Dissolve bouillon granules in hot water. Add to crumb mixture; mix well.

Place beef on board or wax paper. Press stuffing in even layer over beef to within ½ inch of edges. Starting with shorter edge, roll beef tightly. Tie with string at both ends.

In large skillet melt remaining 2 tablespoons Butter Flavor Crisco. Add rolled beef. Brown over medium-high heat. Transfer to oven cooking bag. Combine soup and water; pour over beef. Loosely tie bag. Place in shallow pan. Bake for 1½ to 1¾ hours, or until fork tender. Let stand 15 minutes before slicing. Serve with juices. **4 to 6 servings**

Italian Meat Loaf

2 tablespoons Butter Flavor Crisco
⅓ cup chopped onion
¼ cup chopped celery
¼ cup chopped green pepper
¾ teaspoon Italian seasoning, divided
¼ teaspoon garlic powder
1½ pounds ground beef
1 slice soft white bread, torn into small
   pieces
¼ cup milk
1 egg
¼ teaspoon salt
⅛ teaspoon pepper
½ cup catsup

Preheat oven to 350°F. In small skillet melt Butter Flavor Crisco. Add onion, celery, green pepper, ½ teaspoon Italian seasoning and garlic powder. Cook and stir over medium heat until tender.

In medium mixing bowl crumble beef. Add onion mixture, bread pieces, milk, egg, salt and pepper. Mix well. Press into 9 × 5 × 3-inch loaf pan. Combine catsup and remaining ¼ teaspoon Italian seasoning. Spread over top of loaf. Bake at 350°F for 1 to 1¼ hours, or until set.   **4 to 6 servings**

↑ Mushroom-Filled Meat Loaf

1½ pounds ground beef
½ cup milk
1 egg
2 slices soft white bread, torn into small
   pieces
2 teaspoons dried parsley flakes
1 teaspoon Worcestershire sauce
½ teaspoon salt
¼ teaspoon pepper
¼ teaspoon garlic powder
2 tablespoons Butter Flavor Crisco
¼ cup chopped onion
1 can (4 ounces) sliced mushrooms,
   drained

Preheat oven to 350°F. In large mixing bowl combine beef, milk, egg, bread pieces, parsley flakes, Worcestershire sauce, salt, pepper and garlic powder. Set aside.

In small skillet melt Butter Flavor Crisco. Add onion and mushrooms. Cook and stir over medium heat until onion is tender. Set aside.

On wax paper, pat beef mixture evenly into 10 × 8-inch rectangle. Spread mushroom mixture over beef to within 1 inch of edges. Roll up rectangle tightly, beginning with shorter edge, using wax paper to lift. Press edges and ends to seal. Place loaf seam side down in 9 × 5 × 3-inch loaf pan. Bake at 350°F for 1 to 1¼ hours, or until set and center no longer pink.   **4 to 6 servings**

Oriental Casserole †

2 cups cooked rice
4 tablespoons Butter Flavor Crisco, divided
1 small onion, cut into thin wedges
½ cup chopped carrot
½ cup thinly sliced celery, cut on diagonal
1 clove garlic, minced
1 pound ground beef
1 can (8 ounces) sliced water chestnuts, drained
3 tablespoons all-purpose flour
1⅔ cups water
2 tablespoons soy sauce
1 teaspoon instant beef bouillon granules
¼ teaspoon ground ginger
¼ teaspoon pepper
1 cup chow mein noodles
Soy sauce

Preheat oven to 350°F. Place rice in 2-quart casserole. Set aside.

In medium skillet melt 1 tablespoon Butter Flavor Crisco. Add onion, carrot, celery and garlic. Cook and stir over medium heat until tender. Add to rice.

In medium skillet cook beef over medium heat until browned. Drain fat. Add beef and water chestnuts to rice mixture.

In 1-quart saucepan melt remaining 3 tablespoons Butter Flavor Crisco. Stir in flour. Slowly blend in water. Add soy sauce, bouillon granules, ginger and pepper. Cook and stir constantly until mixture thickens and bubbles. Stir into beef and rice mixture. Top with chow mein noodles. Bake at 350°F for 30 to 35 minutes, or until hot and bubbly. Serve with additional soy sauce.

4 to 6 servings

← Reuben Sandwiches

Sauce:
1 tablespoon Butter Flavor Crisco
¼ cup chopped green pepper
¼ cup chopped onion
½ cup mayonnaise
1 tablespoon catsup
1 teaspoon vinegar
½ teaspoon Worcestershire sauce
¼ teaspoon salt
⅛ teaspoon pepper

Sandwiches:
¼ cup Butter Flavor Crisco, melted
8 slices rye or pumpkernickel bread
2 cups shredded Swiss cheese
1 pound shredded corned beef
1 cup drained sauerkraut

Preheat oven to 350°F. For sauce, in small skillet melt Butter Flavor Crisco. Add green pepper and onion. Cook and stir over medium heat until tender. Transfer to small mixing bowl. Stir in mayonnaise, catsup, vinegar, Worcestershire sauce, salt and pepper. Set aside.

For sandwiches, brush melted Butter Flavor Crisco on one side of each slice of bread. Place 4 slices, greased side down, on foil-lined baking sheet. Spread each with 1 tablespoon sauce. Layer each with ½ cup cheese, ¼ pound corned beef and ¼ cup sauerkraut. Top with remaining 4 slices bread, greased side up. Cover sandwiches with foil and seal tightly.

Bake at 350°F for 15 minutes. Remove foil. Set oven to broil and/or 550°F. Broil 2 to 3 inches from heat for 2 to 5 minutes on each side to toast.

Rachel Sandwiches: Follow the recipe above, omitting sauerkraut. **4 sandwiches**

Veal in Herb Cream Sauce↑

¼ cup plus 3 tablespoons all-purpose flour, divided
¾ teaspoon salt, divided
¼ teaspoon white pepper, divided
1 to 1½ pounds veal cutlets, ¼ inch thick
3 tablespoons Butter Flavor Crisco, divided
1 tablespoon snipped fresh parsley
¼ teaspoon dried tarragon leaves or dried dill weed
1 cup water
½ cup half-and-half
2 tablespoons white wine
1 teaspoon Dijon-style mustard
1 teaspoon instant chicken bouillon granules
1½ cups fresh sliced mushrooms
2 tablespoons chopped green onion
Hot cooked egg noodles

In shallow bowl combine ¼ cup flour, ½ teaspoon salt and ⅛ teaspoon white pepper. Dredge veal cutlets in flour mixture. In large skillet melt 2 tablespoons Butter Flavor Crisco. Add coated veal. Brown both sides over medium heat. Transfer to platter. Cover with foil.

Melt remaining tablespoon Butter Flavor Crisco with drippings in skillet. Remove from heat. Stir in remaining 3 tablespoons flour, ¼ teaspoon salt, ⅛ teaspoon white pepper, parsley and tarragon. Blend in water, half-and-half, wine, mustard and bouillon granules. Cook over medium heat, stirring constantly, until mixture thickens and bubbles. Stir in mushrooms and green onion. Cook until mushrooms are tender. Return veal to sauce and cook for about 2 minutes, or until heated through. Serve over egg noodles.   **4 to 6 servings**

43

Veal in Sour Cream Sauce

2 tablespoons Butter Flavor Crisco
1½ pounds veal stew meat, cut into 1-inch cubes
¼ cup chopped onion
¼ teaspoon fennel seed, crushed
½ teaspoon instant chicken bouillon granules
¼ cup hot water
2 tablespoons snipped fresh parsley
½ teaspoon salt
¼ teaspoon pepper
2 tablespoons all-purpose flour
¼ cup cold water
½ cup dairy sour cream
½ cup half-and-half
1 tablespoon lemon juice
Hot cooked egg noodles

In large skillet melt Butter Flavor Crisco. Add veal, onion and fennel seed. Cook over medium heat until veal is browned. Dissolve bouillon granules in hot water. Add to veal and onions. Stir in parsley, salt and pepper. Reduce heat to medium-low. Cover and cook for about 5 minutes, or until veal is tender, stirring occasionally.

Blend flour and cold water together. Stir into veal. Cook over medium heat, stirring constantly, until mixture thickens and bubbles. Reduce heat to low.

In small bowl combine sour cream, half-and-half and lemon juice. Blend into thickened mixture and cook until heated through. Serve over egg noodles.

4 to 6 servings

Curried Lamb Stew

½ cup all-purpose flour
1 teaspoon salt
¼ teaspoon pepper
1½ to 2 pounds lamb stew meat, cut into 1½-inch cubes
¼ cup Butter Flavor Crisco
2 medium potatoes, cut into 1½-inch cubes
2 medium carrots, cut into ¼-inch slices
1 medium onion, cut into thin wedges
1 large green pepper, cut into large chunks
1 medium apple, peeled and chopped
1 can (16 ounces) whole tomatoes, undrained, cut up
4 cups water
2 tablespoons curry powder
1 tablespoon instant chicken bouillon granules
½ teaspoon ground cinnamon
6 whole cloves
Hot cooked rice

In large plastic food storage bag combine flour, salt and pepper. Add lamb. Shake to coat.

In Dutch oven melt Butter Flavor Crisco. Add coated lamb and any remaining flour. Brown over medium-high heat. Add potatoes, carrots, onion, green pepper, apple, tomatoes and water. Heat to boiling. Add curry powder, bouillon granules, cinnamon and cloves. Reduce heat. Cover and simmer for 1 to 1½ hours, or until vegetables and meat are tender. Remove cloves. Serve with rice.

8 servings

Lamb Meatballs With Herb Tomato Sauce ✝

  2 tablespoons Butter Flavor Crisco
⅓ cup chopped onion
  2 medium cloves garlic, minced, divided
1½ pounds ground lamb
½ cup half-and-half
½ cup snipped fresh parsley
⅓ cup fine dry bread crumbs (unseasoned)
  1 egg
¼ teaspoon salt
⅛ teaspoon pepper
  1 medium green pepper, cut into 1-inch
     chunks
  1 medium zucchini, cut in half lengthwise
     and then into ¼-inch slices
  1 can (15 ounces) tomato sauce
  1 can (14½ ounces) whole tomatoes,
     undrained
  1 teaspoon sugar
  1 teaspoon dried rosemary leaves
     Hot cooked rice

In large skillet melt Butter Flavor Crisco. Add onion and one clove minced garlic. Cook and stir over medium heat until onion is tender. Transfer to medium mixing bowl. Add lamb, half-and-half, parsley, bread crumbs, egg, salt and pepper. Shape into 16 meatballs. Place in large skillet. Cook over medium heat until browned on all sides. Remove meatballs and set aside.

Drain all but 1 tablespoon fat from skillet. Add green pepper and zucchini. Cook and stir over medium heat for about 15 minutes, or until tender. Add tomato sauce, tomatoes, sugar, rosemary and remaining minced garlic. Heat to boiling, stirring to break apart tomatoes. Reduce heat. Add meatballs. Simmer, uncovered, for 15 to 20 minutes, or until meatballs are firm and sauce is reduced and slightly thickened. Serve with rice. **4 servings**

← Creole Pork Chops

¼ cup Butter Flavor Crisco, divided
8 pork chops, ½ inch thick
⅓ cup chopped onion
⅓ cup chopped celery
¼ cup chopped green pepper
1 large clove garlic, minced
2 cups crumbled corn bread
1 egg, slightly beaten
1 can (8 ounces) whole tomatoes, undrained, cut up
1 can (8 ounces) tomato sauce
1 teaspoon packed brown sugar
½ teaspoon chili powder
¼ teaspoon salt
⅛ teaspoon pepper
⅛ teaspoon cayenne
1 bay leaf

Preheat oven to 350°F. In large skillet melt 2 tablespoons Butter Flavor Crisco. Add 4 chops. Brown both sides over medium heat. Repeat with remaining chops. Remove from skillet and set aside.

In large skillet combine remaining 2 tablespoons Butter Flavor Crisco, onion, celery, green pepper and garlic. Cook and stir over medium heat until tender. Remove from heat.

In medium mixing bowl combine corn bread, egg and half of the onion mixture. Set aside.

To remaining mixture in skillet add tomatoes, tomato sauce, brown sugar, chili powder, salt, pepper, cayenne and bay leaf. Simmer, uncovered, for about 10 minutes. Remove from heat. Remove bay leaf.

In 3-quart casserole place 4 pork chops. Spread corn bread mixture over chops. Arrange remaining chops on top. Pour sauce over. Cover. Bake at 350°F for 45 to 55 minutes, or until chops are tender. **4 servings**

Cheese-Stuffed Chicken Breasts →

¼ cup chopped green onion
1 teaspoon dried parsley flakes
¼ teaspoon salt
⅛ teaspoon pepper
⅛ teaspoon garlic powder
4 whole boneless chicken breasts, pounded
   to ⅛-inch thickness
4 slices (1 ounce each) Swiss cheese
¼ cup all-purpose flour
½ cup seasoned fine dry bread crumbs
2 tablespoons grated Parmesan cheese
2 eggs, slightly beaten
½ cup Butter Flavor Crisco

Preheat oven to 375°F. In small mixing bowl combine green onion, parsley flakes, salt, pepper and garlic powder. Set aside.

Place one piece of cheese in center of each chicken breast. Top with one-fourth of onion mixture. Starting at narrow edge, roll each breast tightly, tucking in sides to enclose cheese and onion mixture. Dredge with flour. In small bowl combine bread crumbs and Parmesan cheese. Dip each rolled breast in beaten egg, then in crumb mixture to coat.

In 9 × 9 × 2-inch pan melt Butter Flavor Crisco. Carefully roll coated breasts in Butter Flavor Crisco and arrange in pan. Bake at 375°F for 30 to 35 minutes, or until golden brown.   **4 servings**

Oven-Fried Chicken

1 cup corn flake crumbs
2 tablespoons grated Parmesan cheese
1 teaspoon dried parsley flakes
¾ teaspoon garlic salt
½ teaspoon dried basil leaves
¼ teaspoon dried oregano leaves
⅛ teaspoon pepper
   2½- to 3-pound broiler-fryer chicken, cut
   up
½ cup Butter Flavor Crisco, melted

Preheat oven to 400°F.

In shallow bowl mix corn flake crumbs, Parmesan cheese, parsley flakes, garlic salt, basil, oregano and pepper. Dip chicken pieces in melted Butter Flavor Crisco, then in crumb mixture, pressing lightly to coat. Place skin side up in 13 × 9 × 2-inch baking pan. Bake, uncovered, at 400°F for 45 to 50 minutes, or until coating is golden brown and chicken near bone is no longer pink.

4 to 6 servings

47

Chicken in Wine Sauce

2½- to 3-pound broiler-fryer chicken, cut up
Salt and pepper
2 tablespoons Butter Flavor Crisco
¾ cup white wine or chicken broth
½ cup cold water, divided
2 medium carrots, peeled and cut into 1½-inch pieces
2 stalks celery, cut into 1-inch pieces
2 teaspoons dried parsley flakes
¾ teaspoon instant chicken bouillon granules
½ teaspoon dried thyme leaves
¼ teaspoon salt
2 tablespoons all-purpose flour
½ cup half-and-half

Sprinkle chicken pieces lightly with salt and pepper.

In large skillet melt Butter Flavor Crisco. Add chicken; brown over medium-high heat. Turn pieces skin side up. Add wine, ¼ cup water, carrots, celery, parsley flakes, bouillon granules, thyme and ¼ teaspoon salt. Cover and simmer for 1 to 1½ hours, or until vegetables are fork tender and chicken near bone is no longer pink. Transfer meat and vegetables to serving platter. Cover with foil and set aside.

Blend flour and remaining ¼ cup cold water together. Blend into juices in skillet. Add half-and-half. Cook and stir over medium heat until mixture thickens. Serve with chicken.   **4 servings**

Chicken and Biscuit Bake

2 cups cubed cooked chicken or turkey
1½ cups frozen green beans
1 tablespoon Butter Flavor Crisco
1 medium onion, chopped
2 medium carrots, cut into julienne strips
½ cup thinly sliced celery
1½ cups water, divided
¼ cup all-purpose flour
1 teaspoon dried parsley flakes
½ teaspoon dried summer savory leaves
½ teaspoon freeze-dried chives
¼ teaspoon salt
¼ teaspoon pepper
1 can (13 ounces) evaporated milk
1½ teaspoons instant chicken bouillon granules

Biscuits:
1 cup all-purpose flour
1½ teaspoons baking powder
1 teaspoon dried parsley flakes
½ teaspoon freeze-dried chives
2 tablespoons Butter Flavor Crisco
½ cup milk

Preheat oven to 375°F. In 2-quart casserole combine chicken and green beans. Set aside.

In 2-quart saucepan melt Butter Flavor Crisco. Add onion, carrots and celery. Cook and stir over medium heat until onion is tender. Add ½ cup water. Heat to boiling. Reduce heat. Cover and simmer for about 12 minutes, or until carrot is tender. Stir in flour, parsley flakes, summer savory, chives, salt and pepper. Slowly blend in remaining 1 cup water, the evaporated milk and bouillon granules. Cook and stir over medium heat until mixture thickens and bubbles. Remove from heat. Stir into chicken and green beans.

For biscuits, in small mixing bowl combine flour, baking powder, parsley flakes and chives. Cut in Butter Flavor Crisco to form coarse crumbs. Stir in milk. Drop dough by spoonfuls onto casserole to form 6 to 8 biscuits. Bake, uncovered, at 375°F for 35 to 40 minutes, or until bubbly and biscuits are golden brown.   **4 to 6 servings**

Chicken With Herbed Rice ↑

2½- to 3-pound broiler-fryer chicken, cut
  up
Salt and pepper
3 tablespoons Butter Flavor Crisco, divided
⅓ cup chopped celery
¼ cup chopped onion
¾ cup uncooked long-grain rice
¼ cup uncooked wild rice, rinsed
1 cup fresh sliced mushrooms
½ teaspoon ground poultry seasoning
½ teaspoon dried rosemary leaves
1 can (10¾ ounces) chicken broth
2 teaspoons dried parsley flakes
2 tablespoons sliced almonds (optional)

Preheat oven to 350°F. Line a 13 × 9 × 2-inch
baking pan with foil. Set aside.

Sprinkle chicken pieces with salt and pepper. In
large skillet melt 2 tablespoons Butter Flavor Crisco.
Add chicken. Brown over medium-high heat. Set
aside.

In small skillet melt remaining 1 tablespoon Butter
Flavor Crisco. Add celery and onion. Cook and stir
over medium heat until tender. Transfer to prepared
pan. Sprinkle rice, wild rice and mushrooms over
celery and onion. Sprinkle in poultry seasoning and
rosemary. Pour chicken broth over mixture.
Arrange chicken pieces on top. Sprinkle parsley
flakes over chicken. Cover tightly with foil.

Bake at 350°F for about 1¼ hours, or until wild
rice is tender. Uncover; sprinkle with almonds. Bake
for 15 minutes longer to crisp chicken.

4 to 6 servings

Paprika Chicken ✝

3 tablespoons Butter Flavor Crisco
1 medium onion, chopped
1 clove garlic, minced
1½ teaspoons paprika
1¼ cups cold water, divided
1 teaspoon instant chicken bouillon granules
½ teaspoon salt
3 whole boneless chicken breasts, split in half, skin removed
3 tablespoons all-purpose flour
1 cup dairy sour cream
Hot cooked egg noodles

In large skillet melt Butter Flavor Crisco. Add onion, garlic and paprika. Cook and stir over medium heat until onion is tender. Stir in 1 cup water, bouillon granules and salt. Heat to boiling. Add chicken breasts. Cover and simmer for 12 to 15 minutes, or until chicken is no longer pink, turning meat once or twice. Transfer chicken to platter. Cover with foil and set aside.

Blend flour and remaining ¼ cup cold water together. Blend into juices in skillet. Cook and stir over medium heat until mixture thickens and bubbles. Reduce heat. Blend in sour cream. Return chicken to sauce and cook until heated through. Serve over egg noodles. **4 to 6 servings**

Sweet and Spicy Barbecued Chicken →

   4 tablespoons Butter Flavor Crisco, divided
     2½- to 3-pound broiler-fryer chicken, cut
       into 8 pieces
   1 clove garlic, minced
   ⅓ cup chopped onion
   1 can (8 ounces) tomato sauce
   ¼ cup chili sauce
   2 tablespoons honey
   1 tablespoon Worcestershire sauce
   ½ teaspoon salt
   ¼ teaspoon pepper
   ¼ teaspoon chili powder
   ¼ teaspoon celery seed

Preheat oven to 350°F. In large skillet melt 2
tablespoons Butter Flavor Crisco. Add chicken.
Brown over medium-high heat. Place skin side up
in 13 × 9 × 2-inch baking pan. Bake at 350°F for 30
minutes.

Meanwhile, in small saucepan melt remaining 2
tablespoons Butter Flavor Crisco. Add garlic and
onion. Cook and stir over medium heat until onion
is tender. Stir in tomato sauce, chili sauce, honey,
Worcestershire sauce, salt, pepper, chili powder and
celery seed. Remove chicken from oven; drain fat
and juices. Pour sauce over chicken. Bake for 35 to
40 minutes longer, or until chicken near bone is no
longer pink.   **4 to 6 servings**

Basted Roast Turkey

Roast defrosted turkey as directed on package,
basting frequently with melted Butter Flavor Crisco.
Turkey is done when meat thermometer inserted in
thickest part of thigh registers 185°F. For easier
carving, let stand 15 to 20 minutes after removing
from oven.

51

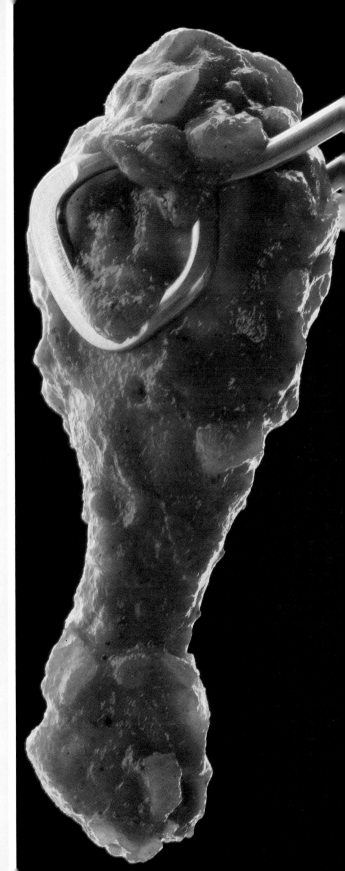

Turkey a la King

⅓ cup Butter Flavor Crisco
⅓ cup chopped green pepper
2 tablespoons chopped green onion
5 tablespoons all-purpose flour
1 teaspoon seasoned salt
⅛ teaspoon pepper
1½ cups milk
¾ cup water
1 teaspoon instant chicken bouillon granules
2 cups cubed cooked turkey or chicken
1 can (8 ounces) mushroom stems and pieces, drained
1 cup frozen peas
1 jar (2 ounces) sliced pimiento, drained
¼ cup sliced or slivered almonds, optional

In 3-quart saucepan melt Butter Flavor Crisco. Add green pepper and onion. Cook and stir over medium heat until tender. Stir in flour, seasoned salt and pepper. Blend in milk, water and bouillon granules. Cook and stir over medium heat for about 10 minutes, or until mixture thickens and bubbles. Stir in turkey, mushrooms, peas and pimiento. Continue cooking for about 5 minutes, or until hot and peas are tender. Serve over toast points or in patty shells. Top with almonds. **4 to 6 servings**

Cornish Hens With Fruit Stuffing

4 Cornish game hens (1¼ to 1½ pounds each), thawed
3 tablespoons Butter Flavor Crisco
¼ cup chopped green onion
1½ cups seasoned croutons
1 small apple, cored and chopped
½ cup chopped walnuts
¼ cup raisins
1 teaspoon grated orange peel, optional
¼ teaspoon dried oregano leaves
¼ teaspoon salt
⅛ teaspoon pepper
½ teaspoon instant chicken bouillon granules
½ cup hot water
Glaze:
2 tablespoons Butter Flavor Crisco, melted
2 tablespoons orange juice
½ teaspoon grated orange peel
1 teaspoon Worcestershire sauce
½ teaspoon dried oregano leaves
¼ teaspoon salt
¼ teaspoon pepper

Preheat oven to 350°F. Remove and discard giblets. Wash hens and pat dry. Set aside.

In small skillet melt Butter Flavor Crisco. Add onion. Cook and stir over medium heat until tender. Transfer to medium mixing bowl. Add croutons, apple, walnuts, raisins, orange peel, oregano, salt and pepper. Dissolve bouillon granules in hot water. Pour over stuffing mixture. Mix well. Stuff hens lightly with stuffing mixture. Use wooden pick to close cavities.

Place hens breast side up in 13×9×2-inch baking pan. Bake at 350°F for 1 hour. Meanwhile, prepare glaze.

For glaze, in small bowl combine melted Butter Flavor Crisco, orange juice and peel, Worcestershire sauce, oregano, salt and pepper. Brush tops of hens with glaze. Bake for 15 to 25 minutes longer, or until golden brown and stuffing registers 185°F on meat thermometer. **4 servings**

Chicken, Ham and Broccoli Crêpes ✝

10 to 12 Dinner-size Crêpes
2/3 cup water
2 cups fresh broccoli pieces (about 1/2
    pound)
2 cups cooked cut-up chicken or turkey
1 cup cubed fully cooked ham (1/2-inch
    cubes)
1/4 cup finely chopped green onion
    Sauce:
1/3 cup Butter Flavor Crisco
1/3 cup all-purpose flour
1 teaspoon salt
1/2 teaspoon dry mustard
1/4 teaspoon dried marjoram leaves
1/8 teaspoon white pepper
3 cups milk
3/4 cup shredded Monterey Jack cheese

Prepare Dinner-size Crêpes as directed, page 109. Set aside. (To prepare a day ahead, stack between wax paper and wrap in plastic wrap; refrigerate.)

Preheat oven to 325°F. In 2-quart saucepan heat water to boiling. Add broccoli; bring to second boil. Reduce heat. Cover and simmer for about 9 minutes, or until tender. Drain. Transfer to large mixing bowl. Add chicken, ham and green onion.

For sauce, in same 2-quart saucepan melt Butter Flavor Crisco. Remove from heat. Stir in flour, salt, dry mustard and white pepper. Slowly blend in milk. Cook over medium heat, stirring constantly, for about 10 minutes, or until mixture thickens and bubbles. Stir in cheese until smooth. Reserve 1 1/2 cups sauce. Add remaining sauce to meat and vegetable mixture. Mix well. Spoon 1/3 cup of mixture down center of each crêpe. Roll to close. Place filled crêpes in 15 1/2 × 10 1/2 × 1-inch jelly roll pan. Pour reserved sauce over crêpes. Bake, uncovered, at 325°F for 25 to 30 minutes, or until heated through.   **4 to 6 servings**

FISH & SEAFOOD

← Pan-Fried Fish Fillets

¾ to 1 cup milk or evaporated milk
1 egg
1½ to 2 cups corn flake crumbs
1 teaspoon salt
⅛ teaspoon pepper
1½ pounds fish fillets, about ½ inch thick, cut into serving-size pieces
3 to 4 tablespoons Butter Flavor Crisco

In shallow dish or pie plate blend milk and egg (use more milk if coating a large number of fillets). Combine corn flake crumbs, salt and pepper. Spread onto plate or waxed paper. Dip fillets in egg mixture, then coat with crumb mixture.

In large skillet melt Butter Flavor Crisco over medium heat. Add a few pieces of fish. Fry for about 4 to 6 minutes, or until golden brown, turning once. Add more Butter Flavor Crisco if needed. Repeat with remaining fish. Place on paper towel-lined plate. Keep warm in 175°F oven.

4 to 6 servings

← Fish and Vegetable Broil

¼ cup Butter Flavor Crisco
1 small onion, chopped
½ cup chopped celery
½ cup chopped green pepper
1 large tomato, seeded and coarsely
  chopped
2 tablespoons seasoned fine dry bread
  crumbs
¼ teaspoon garlic salt
⅛ teaspoon pepper
1 to 1½ pounds fish fillets, about ½ inch
  thick, cut into serving-size pieces
¼ cup grated Parmesan cheese

Preheat oven to broil and/or 550°F. In small skillet melt Butter Flavor Crisco. Add onion, celery and green pepper. Cook and stir over medium heat until tender. Stir in tomato, bread crumbs, garlic salt and pepper. Remove from heat. Set aside.

Broil fish on both sides according to directions for Broiled Fish Fillets, above. Divide and spread vegetable mixture over broiled fish. Sprinkle with Parmesan cheese. Broil 6 inches from heat for 2 to 4 minutes longer, or until golden brown.

4 to 6 servings

Broiled Fish Fillets

¼ to ⅓ cup Butter Flavor Crisco, melted
1 to 1½ pounds fish fillets, about ½ inch
  thick, cut into serving-size pieces

Set rack 4 to 6 inches from broiler. Preheat oven to broil and/or 550°F. Brush broiling pan with melted Butter Flavor Crisco.

Arrange fish in prepared pan. Brush with Butter Flavor Crisco. Broil for 4 to 7 minutes, or until fish flakes easily with fork, turning once. Brush occasionally with Butter Flavor Crisco during cooking. **4 to 6 servings**

Sautéed Scallops →

¼ cup all-purpose flour
½ teaspoon salt
¼ teaspoon pepper
1 pound scallops, rinsed
3 tablespoons Butter Flavor Crisco
1 large clove garlic, cut into 4
    pieces
⅓ cup water
2 tablespoons white wine
1 tablespoon lemon juice
1 tablespoon fresh snipped parsley

In large plastic food storage bag combine flour, salt
and pepper. Add scallops. Shake to coat. Shake off
and discard excess flour. Set coated scallops aside.

In large skillet melt Butter Flavor Crisco. Add garlic.
Cook over medium heat for 1 minute. Remove
garlic and discard. Add coated scallops to skillet.
Cook over medium heat until light golden brown.
Remove from heat. Stir in water, wine, lemon juice
and parsley. Cook over medium heat until mixture
thickens and bubbles and scallops are opaque.
Serve immediately.   **4 servings**

Deep-Fried Frog Legs

1¼ cups all-purpose flour, divided
½ teaspoon salt
¼ teaspoon garlic powder
1 egg
1¼ cups milk, divided
1 pound frog legs, split
    Butter Flavor Crisco for frying

In large bowl combine 1 cup flour, salt and garlic
powder. Add egg and ½ cup milk. Stir with fork to
combine. Blend in remaining ¾ cup milk. Set aside.
Place remaining ¼ cup flour in large plastic bag.
Add frog legs. Shake to coat.

In deep-fat fryer or deep saucepan heat 2 inches
Butter Flavor Crisco to 360°F. Dip coated frog legs
in batter. Fry several pieces at a time for 5 to 6
minutes, or until deep golden brown. Drain on
paper towels.   **4 to 6 servings**

57

Salmon Croquettes ✝

1 can (15½ ounces) salmon, drained,
  cleaned and flaked
1 egg
1 cup corn flake crumbs, divided
2 tablespoons Butter Flavor Crisco
⅓ cup chopped celery
¼ cup chopped onion
1 tablespoon all-purpose flour
¼ teaspoon salt
⅛ teaspoon pepper
¼ cup milk
  Butter Flavor Crisco for frying

In medium bowl combine salmon, egg and ½ cup corn flake crumbs. Mix well. Set aside.

In 1-quart saucepan melt Butter Flavor Crisco. Add celery and onion. Cook and stir over medium heat until tender. Stir in flour, salt and pepper. Blend in milk. Cook and stir over medium heat until mixture thickens and bubbles. Remove from heat. Blend into salmon mixture. Shape by scant ⅓-cupfuls into cone shapes. Roll in remaining corn flake crumbs to coat.

In deep-fat fryer or deep saucepan heat 1½ to 2 inches Butter Flavor Crisco to 350°F. Fry a few pieces at a time in hot oil for 2½ to 3 minutes, or until deep golden brown, turning once or twice. Drain on paper towels. Serve immediately or keep warm in 175°F oven. Serve with *Lemon Dill Sauce*, page 75, if desired.

Tuna Croquettes: Follow the recipe above, substituting 1 can (12½ ounces) tuna for salmon.

4 servings

Shrimp and Vegetable Stir-Fry →

¾ pound medium fresh shrimp, peeled
   and deveined
3 teaspoons cornstarch, divided
⅛ teaspoon ground ginger
   Dash garlic powder
½ pound fresh broccoli
1 quart hot water
1 tablespoon sesame seed (optional)
4 tablespoons Butter Flavor Crisco,
   divided
1 cup cold water
½ teaspoon instant chicken bouillon
   granules
1 package (6 ounces) frozen pea pods,
   thawed

In medium bowl combine shrimp, 1 teaspoon cornstarch, ginger and garlic. Cover and refrigerate.

Remove tough ends of stalk from broccoli. Cut stalk into ¾-inch pieces; cut heads into flowerets. In 2-quart saucepan heat hot water to boiling. Add broccoli. Cover and cook for 1 minute. Remove from heat. Drain and rinse under cold water. Drain and set aside.

Place sesame seed in skillet. Cook over medium heat until golden brown, stirring frequently. Remove from heat. Set aside.

Remove shrimp mixture from refrigerator. In large skillet melt 2 tablespoons Butter Flavor Crisco over medium heat. Add shrimp mixture. Cook and stir until shrimp are opaque. Return to medium mixing bowl. Set aside.

In small bowl blend cold water, remaining 2 teaspoons cornstarch and bouillon granules. Set aside.

In same large skillet melt remaining 2 tablespoons Butter Flavor Crisco. Add broccoli. Cook and stir over medium heat until tender. Add pea pods. Cook and stir for 1 minute longer. Add cornstarch mixture. Cook and stir until mixture begins to bubble. Add shrimp. Cook and stir until mixture thickens and bubbles. Sprinkle with sesame seed before serving. Serve over *rice*, if desired.

4 to 6 servings

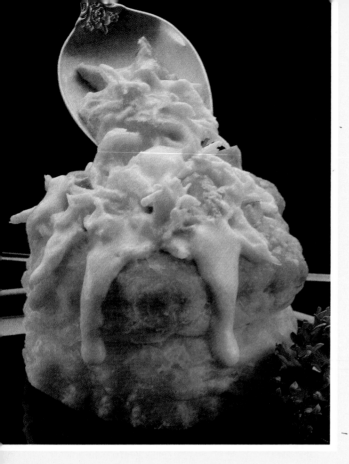

← Crab Newburg

⅓ cup Butter Flavor Crisco
⅓ cup chopped green pepper
¼ cup all-purpose flour
¾ teaspoon salt
¼ teaspoon paprika
3 cups half-and-half
¼ cup sherry (optional)
3 egg yolks, slightly beaten
2 cans (6 ounces each) crab meat, rinsed and drained
2 tablespoons chopped pimiento

In 2-quart saucepan melt Butter Flavor Crisco. Add green pepper. Cook and stir over medium heat until tender. Stir in flour, salt and paprika. Blend in half-and-half and sherry. Cook and stir over medium heat until mixture thickens. Remove from heat. Blend small amount of hot mixture into egg yolks. Return to hot mixture, stirring to combine. Add crab meat and pimiento. Cook and stir over low heat until heated through. Serve in patty shells or over toast points. **8 servings**

Scalloped Oysters

5 tablespoons Butter Flavor Crisco, divided
1½ cups sliced fresh mushrooms
¼ cup finely chopped onion
3 tablespoons all-purpose flour
¼ teaspoon salt
⅛ teaspoon white pepper
½ cup half-and-half
¼ cup dry white wine
¼ cup water
½ teaspoon instant chicken bouillon granules
8 ounces fresh oysters, undrained
½ cup seasoned fine dry bread crumbs
1 teaspoon dried parsley flakes

Preheat oven to 400°F. In medium skillet melt 3 tablespoons Butter Flavor Crisco. Add mushrooms and onion. Cook and stir over medium heat until tender. Stir in flour, salt and white pepper. Slowly blend in half-and-half, wine, water and bouillon granules. Cook and stir over medium heat until mixture thickens and bubbles. Add oysters and liquid. Heat to boiling, stirring constantly. Remove from heat. Spoon mixture into 4 individual baking dishes.

In small saucepan melt remaining 2 tablespoons Butter Flavor Crisco. Remove from heat. Add bread crumbs and parsley flakes, tossing to coat. Divide and sprinkle crumb mixture over top of each baking dish. Bake at 400°F for about 10 minutes, or until bubbly. **4 servings**

Clam and Vegetable Pot Pie ↑

Crust:
1 cup all-purpose flour
½ teaspoon garlic salt
⅓ cup Butter Flavor Crisco
3 to 4 tablespoons cold water

Filling:
2 cans (6½ ounces each) minced clams,
　　¾ cup liquid reserved
2 medium baking potatoes, cut in half
　　lengthwise and thinly sliced
1 cup frozen whole kernel corn
½ cup chopped carrot
⅓ cup chopped celery
⅓ cup chopped green pepper
¼ cup finely chopped onion

Sauce:
3 tablespoons Butter Flavor Crisco
¼ cup all-purpose flour
1 teaspoon dried parsley flakes
¼ teaspoon ground sage
¼ teaspoon dried thyme leaves
¼ teaspoon salt
¼ teaspoon pepper
　　Reserved clam liquid
1 can (5⅓ ounces) evaporated milk

For crust, in medium mixing bowl combine flour and garlic salt. Cut in Butter Flavor Crisco to form coarse crumbs. Add water, 1 tablespoon at a time, mixing with fork until particles are moistened and cling together. Form dough into ball. Set aside.

For filling, in 2-quart casserole combine clams, potatoes, corn, carrot, celery, green pepper and onion. Set aside.

Preheat oven to 375°F. For sauce, in 1-quart saucepan melt Butter Flavor Crisco. Remove from heat. Stir in flour, parsley flakes, sage, thyme, salt and pepper. Slowly blend in reserved clam liquid and evaporated milk. Cook and stir over medium heat until mixture thickens and bubbles. Stir into clam and vegetable mixture.

Roll crust to fit top of casserole. Place over filling and sauce. Flute edge. Make 2 or 3 slits in crust with knife. Bake at 375°F for 60 to 65 minutes, or until crust is light golden brown.　　**4 to 6 servings**

CHEESE EGGS & SAUCES

← Double Cheese Soufflé

⅓ cup Butter Flavor Crisco
¼ cup all-purpose flour
¼ teaspoon salt
⅛ teaspoon pepper
1½ cups milk
1 cup shredded Colby or Cheddar cheese
2 tablespoons grated Parmesan cheese
4 eggs, separated

Preheat oven to 375°F. Grease 1½-quart soufflé dish or casserole. Set aside.

In 2-quart saucepan melt Butter Flavor Crisco. Remove from heat. Stir in flour, salt and pepper. Blend in milk. Cook and stir over medium heat until mixture thickens. Stir in Colby and Parmesan cheese until smooth. Remove from heat and set aside.

In small mixing bowl beat egg yolks at high speed of electric mixer until thick and lemon colored. Blend yolks into thickened mixture. Set aside.

Clean beaters thoroughly. In large mixing bowl beat egg whites at high speed until stiff but not dry. Fold thickened mixture into beaten egg whites. Pour into prepared dish. Bake at 375°F for 30 to 35 minutes, or until golden brown and knife inserted in center comes out clean. Serve immediately. **4 servings**

Miniature Breakfast Quiches †

3 slices bacon, diced
⅓ cup chopped onion
3 eggs
1½ cups half-and-half
1 package (10 ounces) frozen chopped spinach, thawed and thoroughly drained
1½ cups grated Cheddar cheese
1 can (8 ounces) sliced water chestnuts, drained and chopped
12 slices white bread, trimmed
⅓ cup Butter Flavor Crisco, melted
Paprika

Preheat oven to 350°F. In small skillet cook diced bacon until almost crisp. Add onion. Cook and stir over medium heat until onion is tender and bacon is crisp. Remove from heat and set aside.

In large mixing bowl beat eggs. Blend in half-and-half. Stir in drained spinach, cheese, water chestnuts and bacon mixture. Set aside.

Brush one side of each slice of trimmed bread with melted Butter Flavor Crisco. Press one slice, greased side down, into each muffin cup so that corners come up over edges of cup. Spoon about ¼ cup spinach mixture into each bread-lined cup. Sprinkle with paprika. Bake at 350°F for 25 to 30 minutes, or until knife inserted in center comes out clean. **12 servings**

Overnight Breakfast Pie ↑

1¼ cups milk

4 eggs, slightly beaten

8 slices white bread, cut in half diagonally

1 package (10 ounces) frozen chopped broccoli or cut asparagus, thawed and drained

1 cup cubed fully cooked ham (½-inch cubes)

1 recipe Thick White Sauce

1 teaspoon dried parsley flakes

½ teaspoon dried basil leaves

⅛ teaspoon garlic powder

1 cup shredded Swiss cheese

¼ cup grated Parmesan cheese

Grease 9- or 10-inch deep-dish pie plate. Set aside.

In shallow dish blend milk and eggs. Dip 8 halves of bread in egg mixture, coating both sides. Arrange to cover bottom of prepared pie plate. Set aside remaining bread halves and egg mixture.

Spread broccoli over bread layer. Top with ham. Prepare white sauce as directed, page 73. Stir in parsley flakes, basil and garlic powder. Pour over broccoli and ham. Top with Swiss cheese. Dip both sides of remaining bread halves in remaining egg mixture. Arrange to cover top of pie. Cover with plastic wrap. Refrigerate overnight.

Preheat oven to 350°F. Sprinkle top of pie with Parmesan cheese. Bake at 350°F for 45 to 55 minutes, or until puffed and golden brown. Let stand 10 minutes before cutting.   **6 to 8 servings**

Easy Omelets

6 eggs
2 tablespoons milk
¼ teaspoon salt
⅛ teaspoon pepper
2 tablespoons Butter Flavor Crisco, divided

In small bowl or 2-cup measure beat eggs, milk, salt and pepper. Set aside while preparing desired filling.

In 10-inch skillet melt 1 tablespoon Butter Flavor Crisco. Add half of egg mixture. Cook over medium heat without stirring until eggs are set.

Spoon half of filling over one half of omelet. With spatula, carefully loosen other half and fold over filling.

Cook for about 1 minute, or until heated through. Slide onto heated platter. Keep warm in 175°F oven while preparing other omelet.

Repeat with remaining egg mixture and filling. Serve immediately. **2 omelets**

← Denver Omelets

2 tablespoons Butter Flavor Crisco
½ cup chopped green pepper
2 tablespoons finely chopped onion
1 cup cubed fully cooked ham (¼-inch cubes)
⅛ teaspoon pepper
1 recipe Easy Omelets

In small skillet melt Butter Flavor Crisco. Add green pepper and onion. Cook and stir over medium heat until tender, adding ham and pepper during last minute. Prepare omelet as directed above. Use half of filling for each omelet, using slotted spoon to remove from skillet. **2 omelets**

Zucchini-Tomato Omelets ↑

1 tablespoon Butter Flavor Crisco
2 tablespoons finely chopped onion
1 medium zucchini, shredded
1 medium tomato, seeded and chopped
¼ teaspoon garlic salt
Dash pepper
1 recipe Easy Omelets

In large skillet melt Butter Flavor Crisco. Add onion. Cook and stir over medium heat until tender. Add zucchini, tomatoes, garlic salt and pepper. Cook over medium heat, stirring occasionally, until tender. Drain thoroughly. Prepare omelet as directed at left. Use half of filling for each omelet, using slotted spoon to remove from skillet. Serve with *Mornay Sauce*, page 75, if desired. **2 omelets**

Cheese and Mushroom Omelets

2 tablespoons Butter Flavor Crisco
2 cups sliced fresh mushrooms (about 8 ounces)
3 tablespoons chopped green onion
¼ teaspoon dried basil leaves
⅛ teaspoon pepper
1 recipe Easy Omelets
½ cup shredded Cheddar cheese, divided

In small skillet melt Butter Flavor Crisco. Add mushrooms, green onion, basil and pepper. Cook and stir over medium heat until tender. Remove from heat and set aside. Prepare omelet as directed at left. Sprinkle ¼ cup cheese over half of each omelet. Cover with half of vegetables, using slotted spoon to remove from skillet. **2 omelets**

Garden Vegetable Scramble ↑

6 eggs
3 tablespoons milk
¾ teaspoon salt
   Dash pepper
2 tablespoons Butter Flavor Crisco
¼ cup chopped green pepper
½ cup shredded carrot

In medium mixing bowl, blend eggs, milk, salt and pepper. Set aside.

In medium skillet melt Butter Flavor Crisco. Add green pepper. Cook and stir over medium heat until tender. Stir in carrot. Add egg mixture. Cook over medium heat, stirring frequently with spatula, for 3 to 4 minutes, or until desired doneness.

4 to 6 servings

Spiced French Toast →

6 eggs
¼ cup milk
1 teaspoon ground cinnamon
½ teaspoon vanilla
¼ teaspoon salt
¼ teaspoon ground nutmeg
2 to 4 tablespoons Butter Flavor Crisco, divided
8 slices bread

In shallow dish blend eggs, milk, cinnamon, vanilla, salt and nutmeg.

In large skillet melt 2 tablespoons Butter Flavor Crisco. Dip both sides of bread in egg mixture. Place 2 or 3 coated slices in skillet. Cook over medium heat until deep golden brown on both sides. Repeat with remaining slices, adding remaining Butter Flavor Crisco to skillet if necessary.

4 servings

Baked Egg and Toast Cups

6 slices white bread, trimmed
¼ cup Butter Flavor Crisco, melted
6 eggs
½ cup shredded Cheddar cheese
Salt and pepper

Preheat oven to 350°F. Lightly grease 6 muffin cups.

Brush both sides of trimmed bread slices with melted Butter Flavor Crisco. Press one slice bread into each muffin cup so that corners comes up over edges of cup. Bake at 350°F for about 15 minutes, or until lightly toasted. Remove from oven. Break one egg into each toast-lined cup. Top with cheese, dividing equally among 6 cups. Sprinkle with salt and pepper. Bake for 15 to 20 minutes longer, or until eggs are set.

6 servings

Grilled Cheese Sandwiches ↑

4 slices bread
3 tablespoons Butter Flavor Crisco, divided
2 slices (¾ ounce each) American cheese
2 slices (¾ ounce each) mozzarella cheese

Spread each slice of bread with about 2 teaspoons Butter Flavor Crisco. Place one slice American and one slice mozzarella cheese between two slices of bread, with Butter Flavor Crisco on the outside. Heat large skillet over medium heat. Cook sandwiches on both sides until golden brown. Serve immediately. **2 sandwiches**

Fried Eggs

Melt 1 to 2 tablespoons Butter Flavor Crisco in skillet. Break each egg into a measuring cup or saucer. Carefully add eggs one at a time to skillet. Cook over low heat until whites are set. Turn eggs gently or cover. Continue cooking to desired doneness. Season with salt and pepper.

	1st Side	2nd Side
1 egg	45 seconds to 1 minute	1 to 2 minutes
2 eggs	2 to 3 minutes	1 to 1½ minutes
4 eggs	3 to 4 minutes	2 to 3 minutes

Apricot Brunch Soufflé →

⅓ cup Butter Flavor Crisco
¼ cup all-purpose flour
1½ cups milk
1 jar (12 ounces) apricot preserves, divided
⅛ teaspoon ground cinnamon
  Dash ground nutmeg
4 eggs, separated
1 cup chopped dried apricots
¼ cup brandy

Preheat oven to 350°F. Grease 1½-quart soufflé dish or casserole. Set aside.

In 2-quart saucepan melt Butter Flavor Crisco. Remove from heat. Stir in flour. Blend in milk. Cook and stir over medium heat until mixture thickens. Remove from heat. Stir in ¼ cup apricot preserves, cinnamon and nutmeg. Set aside.

In small mixing bowl beat egg yolks at high speed of electric mixer until thick and lemon colored. Blend yolks into thickened mixture. Fold in dried apricots. Set aside.

Clean beaters thoroughly. In large mixing bowl beat egg whites at high speed until stiff but not dry. Fold thickened mixture into beaten egg whites. Pour into prepared dish. Bake at 350°F for 35 to 40 minutes, or until golden brown and knife inserted in center comes out clean.

Meanwhile, prepare sauce. In 1-quart saucepan combine remaining apricot preserves and brandy. Heat to boiling over medium heat, stirring constantly. Boil for 1 minute. Set aside. Serve with soufflé, immediately after removing from oven.

4 servings

← Macaroni and Cheese

1 package (7 ounces) elbow macaroni
¼ cup Butter Flavor Crisco
3 tablespoons all-purpose flour
½ teaspoon salt
¼ teaspoon onion powder
¼ teaspoon dry mustard
¼ teaspoon curry powder, optional
⅛ teaspoon pepper
1⅔ cups milk
2 cups shredded Cheddar cheese (about 8 ounces)

Topping:
¼ cup Butter Flavor Crisco, melted
⅔ cup fine dry bread crumbs (unseasoned)
1 teaspoon dried parsley flakes

Preheat oven to 350°F. Cook macaroni as directed on package. Drain. Transfer to 2-quart casserole. Set aside.

In small saucepan melt Butter Flavor Crisco. Remove from heat. Stir in flour, salt, onion powder, dry mustard, curry powder and pepper. Gradually blend in milk. Cook and stir over medium heat until mixture thickens and bubbles. Stir in cheese until smooth. Remove from heat. Stir into macaroni.

For topping, combine melted Butter Flavor Crisco, bread crumbs and parsley flakes. Sprinkle over macaroni and cheese. Bake at 350°F for 20 to 25 minutes, or until bubbly.

Spicy Macaroni and Cheese: Follow the recipe above. After cooking macaroni, melt 1 tablespoon Butter Flavor Crisco in small skillet. Add ⅓ cup chopped green pepper and ¼ cup chopped onion. Cook and stir over medium heat until tender. Add to macaroni. Drain 1 can (16 ounces) whole tomatoes. Chop and add to macaroni. Continue as directed, substituting ½ teaspoon chili powder and ⅛ teaspoon ground cumin for dry mustard, onion powder and curry. **4 to 6 servings**

White Sauce ➔

Thin:
1 tablespoon Butter Flavor Crisco
1 tablespoon all-purpose flour
½ teaspoon salt
⅛ teaspoon white or black pepper
1 cup milk

Medium:
2 tablespoons Butter Flavor Crisco
2 tablespoons all-purpose flour
½ teaspoon salt
⅛ teaspoon white or black pepper
1 cup milk

Thick:
3 tablespoons Butter Flavor Crisco
3 tablespoons all-purpose flour
½ teaspoon salt
⅛ teaspoon white or black pepper
1 cup milk

In 1-quart saucepan melt Butter Flavor Crisco. Remove from heat. Stir in flour, salt and pepper. Slowly blend in milk. Cook over medium heat, stirring constantly until mixture thickens and bubbles.

Herb Sauce: Follow the recipe above, adding ¼ teaspoon dried herbs (basil, oregano, thyme, dill, summer savory, etc.) with flour, salt and pepper.

Cheese Sauce: Follow the recipe above, adding ½ cup shredded cheese after mixture thickens. Stir until cheese melts. *Pictured below.*

1 cup sauce

Rich Tarragon Sauce ⭡

2 tablespoons Butter Flavor Crisco
1 tablespoon all-purpose flour
½ teaspoon dried parsley flakes
¼ teaspoon dried tarragon leaves
⅛ teaspoon salt
Dash pepper
⅔ cup half-and-half
1 tablespoon white wine
1 egg yolk, beaten

In 1-quart saucepan melt Butter Flavor Crisco.
Remove from heat. Stir in flour, parsley flakes,
tarragon, salt and pepper. Blend in half-and-half
and wine. Cook over medium heat, stirring
constantly, until mixture thickens and bubbles.
Blend small amount of hot mixture into egg yolk.
Blend back into hot mixture, stirring to combine.
Cook and stir until mixture thickens. Serve
immediately with fish, chicken or beef.

¾ cup sauce

Wine Sauce

2 tablespoons Butter Flavor Crisco
2 tablespoons finely chopped onion
⅔ cup hot water
⅓ cup white wine
¾ teaspoon instant chicken bouillon granules
¼ teaspoon dried rosemary leaves
⅛ teaspoon dried thyme leaves
⅛ teaspoon pepper
1 tablespoon cornstarch
2 tablespoons cold water

In small saucepan melt Butter Flavor Crisco. Add
onion. Cook and stir over medium heat until
tender. Add hot water, wine, bouillon granules,
rosemary, thyme and pepper. Heat to boiling.
Blend cornstarch and cold water together. Blend
into sauce. Return to boil. Cook and stir until
mixture thickens. Serve with fish or poultry.

1 cup sauce

Lemon Dill Sauce †

2 tablespoons Butter Flavor Crisco
1 tablespoon all-purpose flour
1 teaspoon grated lemon peel
¼ teaspoon dried dill weed
¼ teaspoon salt
1 cup half-and-half or milk
1 egg yolk, beaten

In 1-quart saucepan melt Butter Flavor Crisco. Remove from heat. Stir in flour, lemon peel, dill weed and salt. Blend in half-and-half. Cook and stir over medium heat until mixture thickens and just comes to a boil. Remove from heat. Blend small amount of hot mixture into egg yolk. Blend back into hot mixture, stirring to combine. Cook and stir until mixture just comes to a boil. Cook and stir for 1 minute longer. Serve with fish. **1 cup sauce**

Mornay Sauce

2 tablespoons Butter Flavor Crisco
2 tablespoons all-purpose flour
¼ teaspoon salt
⅛ teaspoon white pepper
  Dash ground nutmeg
⅓ cup water
½ teaspoon instant chicken bouillon granules
⅔ cup half-and-half
¼ cup shredded Swiss cheese

In small saucepan melt Butter Flavor Crisco. Remove from heat. Stir in flour, salt, white pepper and nutmeg. Slowly blend in water, bouillon granules and half-and-half. Cook over medium heat, stirring constantly, until mixture thickens and bubbles. Stir in cheese until smooth. Serve with vegetables or eggs. **1¼ cups sauce**

VEGETABLES

← Summer Vegetable Sauté

3 tablespoons Butter Flavor Crisco
1 medium onion, thinly sliced and
   separated into rings
1 clove garlic, minced
1 pound zucchini (about 4 small), cut
   into $2\frac{1}{2} \times \frac{1}{2}$-inch strips
1 cup sliced fresh mushrooms
10 cherry tomatoes, cut in half lengthwise
$\frac{1}{2}$ teaspoon salt
$\frac{1}{4}$ teaspoon dried oregano leaves
$\frac{1}{8}$ teaspoon pepper

In large skillet melt Butter Flavor Crisco. Add onion
and garlic. Cook and stir over medium heat until
onion is tender. Add zucchini and mushrooms.
Cook for 10 to 12 minutes, stirring occasionally.
Add tomatoes, salt, oregano and pepper. Cook for
2 to 3 more minutes, or until zucchini is tender.
Sprinkle with *Parmesan cheese* before serving, if
desired. **4 to 6 servings**

← Green Beans Amandine

¼ cup plus 3 tablespoons Butter Flavor
    Crisco, divided
1 package (2½ ounces) slivered almonds
⅔ cup fine dry bread crumbs
    (unseasoned)
1 pound fresh green beans, cut into
    1-inch pieces (about 4 cups)
½ cup water
1 teaspoon salt, divided
2 tablespoons all-purpose flour
¼ teaspoon dried marjoram leaves
⅛ teaspoon onion powder
⅛ teaspoon pepper
1 cup milk

Preheat oven to 350°F. Lightly grease 1½-quart
casserole.

In small skillet melt 1 tablespoon Butter Flavor
Crisco. Stir in almonds. Cook over medium heat.
stirring constantly, for 2 to 3 minutes, or until light
golden brown. Remove from heat. Transfer to
prepared casserole. Set aside.

In small skillet melt ¼ cup Butter Flavor Crisco.
Remove from heat. Stir in bread crumbs. Set aside.

In 2-quart saucepan combine green beans, water
and ½ teaspoon salt. Heat to boiling. Reduce heat;
cover and simmer for 7 to 8 minutes, or until
tender. Drain. Add to almonds.

In 2-quart saucepan melt remaining 2 tablespoons
Butter Flavor Crisco. Remove from heat. Stir in
flour, remaining ½ teaspoon salt, marjoram, onion
powder and pepper. Gradually blend in milk. Cook
and stir over medium heat for 4 to 5 minutes, or
until mixture thickens. Remove from heat. Stir into
green beans and almonds. Sprinkle prepared
crumbs on top. Bake, uncovered, at 350°F for 20
to 25 minutes, or until bubbly and golden brown.

4 to 6 servings

Cabbage and Noodles ↑

2 cups uncooked egg noodles
¼ cup plus 1 tablespoon Butter Flavor Crisco, divided
⅓ cup chopped onion
3 cups coarsely shredded cabbage (about ¾ pound)
¼ teaspoon fennel seed
2 tablespoons snipped fresh parsley
½ teaspoon salt
¼ teaspoon pepper

Prepare noodles according to package directions, adding 1 tablespoon Butter Flavor Crisco to cooking water. Drain. Set aside.

In large skillet melt remaining ¼ cup Butter Flavor Crisco. Add onion. Cook and stir over medium heat until tender. Add cabbage and fennel seed. Cook and stir over medium heat until tender. Transfer to medium serving bowl. Add noodles, parsley, salt and pepper. Toss well.

4 to 6 servings

Herbed Brussels Sprouts and Carrots

1 cup thinly sliced carrots
1 package (8 to 10 ounces) frozen Brussels sprouts
3 tablespoons Butter Flavor Crisco
½ cup sliced green onion (½-inch slices)
1 clove garlic, minced
½ teaspoon lemon juice
⅛ teaspoon dried rosemary leaves
Dash pepper

Add carrots to Brussels sprouts and cook as directed on Brussels sprouts package. Drain. Set aside.

In large skillet melt Butter Flavor Crisco. Cook and stir green onion and garlic over medium heat until onion is tender. Stir in lemon juice, rosemary and pepper. Add drained Brussels sprouts and carrots. Cook and stir for about 2 minutes, or until heated through.

4 to 6 servings

← Italian Rice and Vegetables

        5 tablespoons Butter Flavor Crisco,
            divided
        1 cup uncooked long-grain rice
        ½ cup broken uncooked spaghetti
            (1-inch pieces)
        ½ teaspoon Italian seasoning
        ½ teaspoon salt
        ⅛ teaspoon pepper
        2 cups hot water
        1 package (10 ounces) frozen chopped
            broccoli, thawed
        1 cup sliced fresh mushrooms
        ¾ cup quartered cherry tomatoes

In 2-quart saucepan melt 3 tablespoons Butter
Flavor Crisco. Add uncooked rice and spaghetti.
Cook and stir over medium heat until rice and
noodles are golden brown. Stir in Italian seasoning,
salt, pepper and hot water. Heat to boiling. Reduce
heat. Cover and simmer for about 15 minutes, or
until water is absorbed. Set aside.

In large skillet melt remaining 2 tablespoons Butter
Flavor Crisco. Add broccoli, mushrooms and
tomatoes. Cook and stir over medium heat until
mushrooms are tender. Add rice mixture. Cook and
stir until heated through.   **6 servings**

Sweet and Sour Beets

        2 tablespoons Butter Flavor Crisco
        1 small onion, thinly sliced and
            separated into rings
        2 tablespoons packed brown sugar
        2 tablespoons honey
        2 tablespoons cider vinegar
        ⅛ teaspoon pepper
        2 cans (16 ounces each) sliced
            beets, drained

In 2-quart saucepan melt Butter Flavor Crisco. Add
onion rings. Cook and stir over medium heat until
tender. Remove from heat. Stir in brown sugar,
honey, vinegar and pepper. Add beets, stirring to
coat. Cook over medium heat until heated through.
        4 to 6 servings

Mexican-Style Corn →

2 tablespoons Butter Flavor Crisco
⅓ cup chopped onion
1 package (16 ounces) frozen corn
1 medium tomato, chopped
1 can (4 ounces) diced green chilies,
   rinsed and drained
2 tablespoons water
   Dash garlic powder

In 2-quart saucepan melt Butter Flavor Crisco. Add onion. Cook and stir over medium heat until tender. Stir in corn, tomato, green chilies, water and garlic powder. Cover and cook over medium heat for 7 minutes, stirring occasionally. Uncover and continue cooking for about 3 minutes, or until hot.

4 to 6 servings

Scalloped Corn

¼ cup Butter Flavor Crisco, divided
⅓ cup chopped onion
⅓ cup chopped celery
2 tablespoons all-purpose flour
¼ teaspoon salt
⅛ teaspoon pepper
1 can (5⅓ ounces) evaporated milk
1 package (10 ounces) frozen whole
   kernel corn
1 egg, slightly beaten
½ cup cracker crumbs

Preheat oven to 350°F. Grease 1-quart casserole. Set aside.

In 1-quart saucepan melt 2 tablespoons Butter Flavor Crisco. Add onion and celery. Cook and stir over medium heat until tender. Stir in flour, salt and pepper. Blend in evaporated milk. Cook and stir until mixture just thickens. Stir in corn and egg. Pour into prepared casserole. Set aside.

In 1-quart saucepan melt remaining 2 tablespoons Butter Flavor Crisco. Stir in cracker crumbs. Sprinkle on top of corn. Bake at 350°F for 25 to 35 minutes, or until golden brown. Garnish with *parsley*, if desired.

4 servings

Carrot Patties ↑

2 cups shredded carrots (3 to 4 medium)
2 eggs
2 tablespoons milk
¼ teaspoon Worcestershire sauce
2 tablespoons finely chopped green onion
2 tablespoons dry seasoned bread crumbs
½ teaspoon salt
⅛ teaspoon pepper
4 to 6 tablespoons Butter Flavor Crisco, divided

In medium mixing bowl combine carrots, eggs, milk, Worcestershire sauce, onion, bread crumbs, salt and pepper. Mix thoroughly.

In large skillet melt 2 to 3 tablespoons Butter Flavor Crisco over medium heat. For each patty, drop about ⅓ cup carrot mixture into pan, flattening slightly with spatula. Fry three patties at a time. Cook for 3 to 4 minutes, or until first side is golden brown and set. Turn; cook for another 2 to 3 minutes, or until other side is golden brown. Fry remaining three patties in remaining 2 to 3 tablespoons Butter Flavor Crisco. Drain on paper towels. **6 servings**

Cauliflower Pie

Pastry:

1¾ cups all-purpose flour
⅓ cup grated Cheddar cheese
½ teaspoon salt ·
½ cup Butter Flavor Crisco
4 to 5 tablespoons water

Filling:

½ cup water
½ teaspoon salt
1 2-pound head cauliflower, cut into
   flowerets (about 6 cups)
⅔ cup grated Cheddar cheese
¼ cup plus 2 tablespoons all-purpose
   flour, divided
2 tablespoons Butter Flavor Crisco
½ teaspoon dried parsley flakes
¼ teaspoon dried basil
¼ teaspoon salt
⅛ teaspoon pepper
½ teaspoon prepared mustard
¾ cup milk

Preheat oven to 425°F. For pastry, in medium mixing bowl combine flour, cheese and salt. Cut in Butter Flavor Crisco to form coarse crumbs. Add water, 1 tablespoon at a time, mixing with fork until particles are moistened and cling together. Form dough into ball. Refrigerate while preparing filling.

For filling, heat water to boiling. Add salt and cauliflower. Cover and simmer for about 5 minutes, or until tender. Drain. Add cheese and 2 tablespoons flour, tossing to coat. Set aside.

In 1-quart saucepan melt Butter Flavor Crisco. Remove from heat. Stir in remaining ¼ cup flour, parsley flakes, basil, salt, pepper and mustard. Gradually blend in milk. Cook and stir over medium heat for 4 to 5 minutes, or until mixture thickens and bubbles. Remove from heat. Stir into cauliflower. Set aside. Continue as directed below.

6 to 8 servings

How to Assemble Cauliflower Pie

Divide prepared dough in half. Roll half of dough 2 inches larger than inverted 9-inch pie pan; fit into pan.

Pour cauliflower mixture into pastry-lined pan. Roll remaining dough to form top crust. Cut slits so steam can escape. Place over cauliflower.

Trim, seal and flute edge. Bake at 425°F for 25 to 30 minutes, or until golden brown. Let stand for 10 minutes before serving.

← Spinach Puff

1 package (10 ounces) frozen chopped
    spinach, thawed and thoroughly
    drained
¼ cup Butter Flavor Crisco
⅓ cup chopped onion
¼ cup all-purpose flour
¼ teaspoon dried dill weed
¼ teaspoon salt
⅛ teaspoon pepper
1 cup half-and-half
1 cup shredded Cheddar cheese
3 eggs, separated

Preheat oven to 350°F. Press all excess moisture
from spinach. Set aside.

Lightly grease 1-quart casserole or soufflé dish. Set
aside.

In 1-quart saucepan melt Butter Flavor Crisco. Add
onion. Cook and stir over medium heat until
tender. Stir in flour, dill weed, salt and pepper.
Blend in half-and-half. Cook and stir over medium
heat until mixture thickens and bubbles. Stir in
cheese until smooth. Remove from heat and set
aside.

In medium mixing bowl beat egg whites at high
speed of electric mixer until stiff but not dry. Set
aside.

In small bowl beat egg yolks slightly. Add small
amount of thickened sauce to egg yolks. Return to
sauce, stirring to combine. Stir in spinach. Fold in
beaten egg whites. Pour into prepared dish. Bake at
350°F for 30 to 40 minutes, or until golden brown
and knife inserted in center comes out clean. Serve
immediately.

Broccoli Puff: Follow the recipe above, substituting
1 package (10 ounces) frozen chopped broccoli,
thawed, for spinach. Add about 5 minutes to
cooking time, if needed.   **4 to 6 servings**

Vegetable-Stuffed Green Peppers ↑

3 medium green peppers
2 tablespoons Butter Flavor Crisco
¼ cup chopped green onion
¼ cup finely chopped celery
1 cup cooked rice
1 medium tomato, seeded and chopped
1 teaspoon dried parsley flakes
¾ teaspoon salt
½ teaspoon chili powder
⅛ teaspoon ground cumin
   Dash cayenne
2 tablespoons prepared chili sauce
1 tablespoon catsup
½ teaspoon sugar
¼ teaspoon Worcestershire sauce
6 slices Monterey Jack cheese
   (3 × 1½-inch)
¼ cup water

Preheat oven to 350°F. Cut green peppers in half lengthwise to make six pieces. Remove seeds and core. In large saucepan boil enough water to cover green peppers. Add peppers; boil for 4 minutes. Drain. Rinse with cold water. Set aside.

In small skillet melt Butter Flavor Crisco. Add green onion and celery. Cook and stir over medium heat until tender. Remove from heat. Transfer to medium mixing bowl. Stir in rice, tomato, parsley flakes, salt, chili powder, cumin and cayenne. Fill green pepper halves with rice mixture. Place in 9 × 9 × 2-inch pan.

In small bowl combine chili sauce, catsup, sugar and Worcestershire sauce. Spoon over top of each filled green pepper. Top each with slice of cheese. Pour water in bottom of pan. Bake, uncovered, at 350°F for 25 to 30 minutes, or until heated and cheese melts.   **4 to 6 servings**

← Twice-Baked Potatoes

4 medium baking potatoes
⅓ cup Butter Flavor Crisco
¼ cup chopped onion
1 teaspoon dried parsley flakes
¼ teaspoon salt
⅛ teaspoon pepper
1½ cups shredded Cheddar cheese
⅓ cup milk
Paprika

Preheat oven to 375°F. Scrub and prick potatoes. Bake at 375°F for 1 to 1¼ hours, or until fork tender. Cool slightly. Reduce oven temperature to 350°F.

Cut thin slice from top of each potato. Scoop out inside, leaving a thin shell. Place scooped-out potato in medium mixing bowl. Place shells in 8 × 8 × 2-inch baking pan. Set aside.

In 1-quart saucepan melt Butter Flavor Crisco. Add onion. Cook and stir over medium heat until tender. Stir in parsley flakes, salt and pepper. Remove from heat. Add to potatoes.

Add Cheddar cheese and milk. Beat at medium speed of electric mixer until light and fluffy, adding more milk to reach desired consistency, if necessary. Spoon mixture back into shells. Sprinkle with paprika. Bake at 350°F for 20 to 25 minutes, or until golden brown.   **4 servings**

Baked Potato Wedges

3 large baking potatoes
¼ cup Butter Flavor Crisco, melted
Paprika
Salt and pepper

Preheat oven to 425°F. Wash and scrub potatoes. Cut lengthwise into quarters. Dip potato pieces in melted Butter Flavor Crisco. Place cut side down in 13 × 9 × 2-inch pan. Bake at 425°F for 30 to 35 minutes, or until fork tender. Sprinkle with paprika, salt and pepper. Serve with *sour cream,* if desired.

4 to 6 servings

86

Rutabaga Au Gratin →

½ cup Butter Flavor Crisco, divided
4 cups shredded rutabaga
2 tablespoons all-purpose flour
¼ teaspoon salt
⅛ teaspoon pepper
1¾ cups milk
½ cup shredded Cheddar cheese
⅔ cup fine dry bread crumbs
 (unseasoned)

Preheat oven to 350°F. Lightly grease 1-quart casserole. Set aside.

In large skillet melt 2 tablespoons Butter Flavor Crisco. Add rutabaga, tossing to coat. Cook and stir over medium heat for about 5 minutes. Remove from heat. Set aside.

In 2-quart saucepan melt 2 tablespoons Butter Flavor Crisco. Remove from heat. Stir in flour, salt and pepper. Blend in milk. Cook and stir over medium heat until mixture thickens. Stir in cheese and rutabaga. Transfer to prepared casserole.

In small saucepan melt remaining ¼ cup Butter Flavor Crisco. Add bread crumbs, tossing to coat. Sprinkle over rutabaga. Bake at 350°F for 25 to 30 minutes, or until bubbly and golden brown.

Turnips Au Gratin: Follow the recipe above, substituting shredded turnips for the rutabaga.
4 to 6 servings

Hashed Brown Potatoes

1½ pounds baking potatoes (about 4
 medium), peeled and shredded
2 tablespoons grated onion
¾ teaspoon salt
⅛ teaspoon pepper
3 tablespoons Butter Flavor Crisco

Rinse and drain potatoes thoroughly. In medium mixing bowl combine potatoes, onion, salt and pepper. Mix well.

In large skillet melt Butter Flavor Crisco. Add potatoes; spread evenly in pan. Cook over medium-high heat for 13 to 15 minutes, or until golden brown and tender, turning potatoes with spatula after half the time. **4 to 6 servings**

Fried Eggplant

1 large eggplant (about 2 pounds)
½ cup all-purpose flour
½ cup yellow corn meal
¼ teaspoon garlic powder
½ teaspoon salt
¼ cup grated Parmesan cheese
½ cup milk
1 egg
½ cup Butter Flavor Crisco

Slice eggplant crosswise into ½-inch slices. Set aside.

In medium bowl combine flour, corn meal, garlic powder, salt and Parmesan cheese. Set aside. In shallow dish blend milk and egg. Set aside.

In large skillet melt Butter Flavor Crisco. Dip each slice of eggplant in milk mixture, then in corn meal mixture to coat. Fry a few at a time over medium heat until golden brown, turning once. Drain on paper towel-lined platter. If needed, add more Butter Flavor Crisco to skillet. Sprinkle with additional *Parmesan cheese* before serving, if desired. **4 to 6 servings**

↑ Fettuccini With Mushrooms

8 ounces uncooked fettuccini
5 tablespoons Butter Flavor Crisco, divided
1 cup sliced fresh mushrooms
2 tablespoons all-purpose flour
½ teaspoon dried parsley flakes or 1 teaspoon snipped fresh parsley
¼ teaspoon onion powder
¼ teaspoon salt
⅛ teaspoon pepper
1¾ cups half-and-half
⅓ cup grated Parmesan cheese

Prepare fettuccini according to package directions, adding 1 tablespoon Butter Flavor Crisco to cooking water. Drain and rinse with warm water. Toss with 1 tablespoon Butter Flavor Crisco. Set aside.

In 2-quart saucepan melt remaining 3 tablespoons Butter Flavor Crisco. Add mushrooms. Cook and stir over medium heat until tender. Stir in flour, parsley flakes, onion powder, salt and pepper. Blend in half-and-half. Cook and stir over medium heat until mixture thickens slightly. Remove from heat. Add fettuccini and Parmesan cheese, tossing to coat. **4 to 6 servings**

Sweet Potato Dressing ↑

1 pound sweet potatoes (about 3
   medium), peeled and cut into 2-inch
   chunks
1 teaspoon salt, divided
¼ cup plus 2 tablespoons Butter Flavor
   Crisco, divided
1 cup chopped celery
¼ cup chopped onion
¼ teaspoon poultry seasoning
¼ teaspoon pepper
½ pound ground seasoned pork
   sausage
3 cups seasoned croutons
1 medium apple, cored and chopped
¼ cup raisins
1 egg, slightly beaten
⅓ cup hot water
½ teaspoon instant chicken bouillon
   granules

Place sweet potatoes in 2-quart saucepan. Add ½
teaspoon salt and enough water to cover. Heat to
boiling. Cover and simmer for 20 to 25 minutes, or
until fork tender. Drain. Set aside to cool.

Preheat oven to 350°F. Lightly grease 2-quart
casserole. Set aside.

In large skillet melt 2 tablespoons Butter Flavor
Crisco. Add celery and onion. Cook and stir over
medium heat until tender. Stir in remaining ½
teaspoon salt, poultry seasoning and pepper.
Transfer to large mixing bowl.

In large skillet brown sausage, stirring to break
apart. Drain if necessary. Add to celery and onion.
Stir in croutons, apple and raisins. Mix in egg.

Melt remaining ¼ cup Butter Flavor Crisco.
Dissolve bouillon granules in hot water. Add melted
Butter Flavor Crisco and bouillon to sausage
mixture. Cut cooked sweet potatoes into ½-inch
cubes. Add to other ingredients. Mix well. Transfer
to prepared casserole. Bake, uncovered, at 350°F
for 35 to 40 minutes, or until golden brown.

8 to 10 servings

BREADS

← Herb Cheese Bread

1 recipe Buttery Bread Dough
1 to 2 teaspoons dried basil leaves or
  dill weed
1½ cups grated sharp Cheddar cheese

Prepare dough as directed, page 92, adding basil
and cheese with last addition of flour.

After kneading, shape dough into round shape.
Place in well-greased 1-quart round casserole. Turn
dough over. Slash top with "X" in center. Cover;
let rise in warm place until doubled, about 1 hour.
(Let dough rise only once.)

Preheat oven to 350°F. Bake at 350°F for 40 to 45
minutes, or until deep golden brown.   **1 round loaf**

Buttery Bread Dough †

1 package active dry yeast
¼ cup warm water (110° - 115°F)
½ cup warm milk (110° - 115°F)
¼ cup Butter Flavor Crisco
1 egg
2 tablespoons sugar
1 teaspoon salt
2½ to 3 cups all-purpose flour

Test dough by pressing in fingertip ½ inch.
Indentation will remain if dough has doubled.

In large mixing bowl combine yeast and water. Add warm milk, Butter Flavor Crisco, egg, sugar, salt and 1½ cups flour. Beat on low speed of electric mixer for 3 minutes. Gradually mix in enough remaining flour to make dough easy to handle.

On well-floured board knead for 5 minutes, or until smooth and elastic, adding flour to board as needed. Shape dough into ball. Place in greased bowl. Turn dough over. Cover; let rise in warm place until doubled, about 1 hour. Punch down dough. Shape as directed in recipe.

NOTE: Kneading may be omitted when making Dinner Rolls, if desired.

Basic Loaf: Form into loaf. Place in well-greased 9 × 5 × 3-inch loaf pan. Cover; let rise in warm place until doubled, about 1 hour. Bake at 375° for 30 to 35 minutes, or until light golden brown.

1 loaf

Dinner Rolls →

1 recipe Buttery Bread Dough

Prepare dough as directed at left. Shape as directed in desired variation, below. Cover; let rise in warm place until doubled, 45 to 60 minutes. Preheat oven to 400°F. Brush tops with melted Butter Flavor Crisco. Bake as directed below. Remove from pan. Cool on wire rack.

Pictured, top to bottom:

Pan Rolls: Thoroughly grease $13 \times 9 \times 2$-inch pan. Divide dough into twenty pieces. Shape into balls. Place in prepared pan. Let rise as directed above. Bake for 7 to 10 minutes, or until golden brown.
20 rolls

Cloverleaf Rolls: Thoroughly grease muffin cups. Divide dough into twelve pieces; divide each piece into thirds. Shape into balls. Place three balls in each prepared muffin cup. Let rise as directed above. Bake for 7 to 10 minutes, or until golden brown.
12 rolls

Herb Pinwheels: Thoroughly grease 9-inch round cake pan. Set aside. On floured board roll dough into a 16×10-inch rectangle. Brush with 2 tablespoons melted Butter Flavor Crisco; sprinkle with 2 teaspoons caraway seed, poppy seed or Italian seasoning. Starting with longer edge, roll dough tightly. Pinch edge into roll to seal. Stretch roll to make even. Cut into sixteen 1-inch slices. Place in prepared pan. Let rise as directed above. Bake for 15 to 20 minutes, or until golden brown.
16 rolls

Cheese Crescents: Thoroughly grease baking sheet. Set aside. Divide dough in half. On floured board roll each half into a 10-inch circle, brush with 1 tablespoon melted Butter Flavor Crisco, and sprinkle with 2 tablespoons grated Parmesan cheese. Cut each circle into eight wedges. Starting with wide ends, roll wedges to point. Place point end down on prepared baking sheet. Pull ends toward centers of rolls to form crescent shape. Let rise as directed above. Bake for 7 to 10 minutes, or until golden brown.
16 rolls

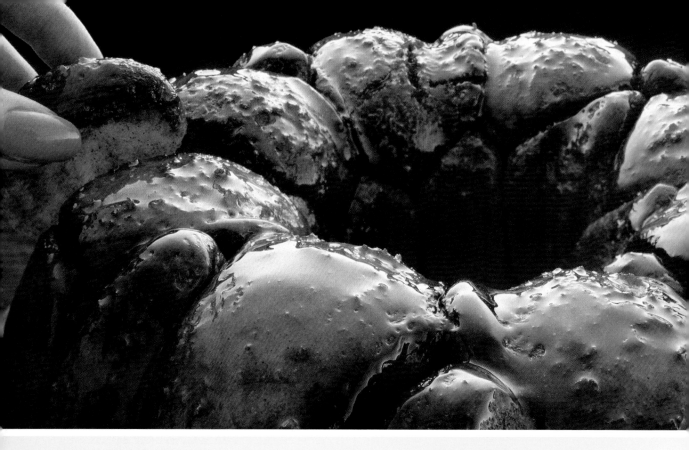

Buttery Sweet Dough

   1 package active dry yeast
  ¼ cup warm water (110° - 115°F)
  ½ cup warm milk (110° - 115°F)
  ¼ cup sugar
  ¾ teaspoon salt
  ¼ cup Butter Flavor Crisco
  1 egg
2½ to 3½ cups all-purpose flour

In large mixing bowl dissolve yeast in warm water. Stir in warm milk, sugar, salt, Butter Flavor Crisco, egg and 1½ cups flour. Stir until smooth. Mix in enough remaining flour to make dough easy to handle.

On well-floured board knead dough for about 5 minutes, or until smooth and elastic, adding flour to board as needed. Shape dough into ball. Place in greased bowl. Turn dough over. Cover; let rise in warm place until doubled, about 1½ to 2 hours. Punch down dough. Shape as directed in recipe.

Monkey Bread ✝

   1 recipe Buttery Sweet Dough
  ⅓ cup granulated sugar
  ⅓ cup packed brown sugar
  1 teaspoon ground cinnamon
  ½ cup finely chopped nuts or coconut
      (optional)
  ⅓ cup Butter Flavor Crisco, melted

Prepare dough as directed, at left. Grease 12-cup fluted ring pan. Set aside.

Divide dough into thirty pieces with sharp knife. In small bowl, mix granulated sugar, brown sugar and cinnamon. Stir in nuts. Coat each piece of dough with melted Butter Flavor Crisco, then with sugar mixture. Layer in prepared pan. Cover; let rise in warm place until doubled, about 1 hour.

Preheat oven to 350°F. Bake for 30 to 40 minutes, or until golden brown. Immediately turn onto serving plate. **1 coffee cake**

Almond Coffee Ring →

1 recipe Buttery Sweet Dough
2 tablespoons Butter Flavor Crisco
3 tablespoons dairy sour cream
1 tablespoon sugar
½ teaspoon almond extract
1 egg
1 tablespoon milk

Glaze:
½ cup confectioners' sugar
1 tablespoon dairy sour cream
1 tablespoon milk

Prepare Buttery Sweet Dough as directed, at left. Lightly grease baking sheet. Set aside.

On floured board roll dough into a 15 × 10-inch rectangle. Spread Butter Flavor Crisco evenly over dough. Mix sour cream, sugar and almond extract. Spread evenly over rectangle. Starting with longer edge, roll dough tightly. Pinch edge into roll to seal. Place seam side down on prepared baking sheet.

Form roll into circle, pinching edges together. With scissors, cut two-thirds of the way through ring at 1- to 1½-inch intervals. Turn each section on its side. Cover; let rise in warm place until doubled, 30 to 45 minutes.

Preheat oven to 350°F. Blend egg and milk; brush on ring. Bake at 350°F for 25 to 35 minutes, or until deep golden brown.

For glaze, combine confectioners' sugar, sour cream and milk. Stir until smooth. Drizzle over coffee ring. Sprinkle with *sliced almonds*, if desired.

1 coffee cake

Cut two-thirds of the way through ring at even intervals, turning each section on its side.

95

Caramel Rolls ↑

1 recipe Buttery Sweet Dough
¼ cup plus 5 tablespoons Butter Flavor
   Crisco, divided
½ cup packed brown sugar
1 to 2 tablespoons milk
⅔ cup chopped nuts (optional)
5 tablespoons granulated sugar
1 tablespoon ground cinnamon

For perfectly-shaped rolls, cut slices with
heavy-duty thread held taut with both hands.

Prepare dough as directed, page 94.

In 1-quart saucepan blend ¼ cup Butter Flavor
Crisco and brown sugar. Add 1 tablespoon milk.
Cook and stir over medium heat until bubbly,
adding more milk if desired for consistency. Quickly
spread in 13×9×2-inch pan. Sprinkle nuts over
mixture.

On floured board roll dough into a 15×10-inch
rectangle. Spread 3 tablespoons Butter Flavor
Crisco over dough. In small bowl mix granulated
sugar and cinnamon. Sprinkle evenly over dough.
Starting with longer edge, roll dough tightly. Pinch
edge into roll to seal. Stretch roll to make even. Cut
into twelve even slices. Place slightly apart on top of
caramel mixture in pan. Cover; let rise in warm
place until doubled, about 30 minutes.

Preheat oven to 350°F. Melt remaining 2
tablespoons Butter Flavor Crisco; brush on rolls.
Bake at 350°F for 25 to 30 minutes, or until light
golden brown. Immediately turn onto serving plate.
Let pan stay inverted over rolls for 5 minutes.

1 dozen rolls

Breakfast Griddle Muffins †

1 package active dry yeast
½ cup warm water (110° - 115°F)
¾ cup warm milk (110° - 115°F)
1 tablespoon sugar
1 teaspoon salt
¼ cup Butter Flavor Crisco
1 egg
4 to 4½ cups all-purpose flour
Corn meal

To serve, split with fork and toast. Delicious with jam or honey!

In medium mixing bowl dissolve yeast in warm water. Add warm milk, sugar, salt, Butter Flavor Crisco, egg and 2 cups flour. Beat on low speed of electric mixer for 3 minutes. Gradually stir in enough remaining flour to make very stiff dough. Cover; let rise in warm place until doubled, about 1 to 1¼ hours. Punch down dough; let rest for 15 minutes.

Lightly sprinkle baking sheet with corn meal. Set aside. On floured board roll dough to ½-inch thickness. Cut into rounds with 3-inch floured cutter. Place on prepared baking sheet. Sprinkle tops lightly with corn meal. Cover; let rise in warm place for 30 minutes.

Preheat griddle or electric frying pan to 300°F. Grease with Butter Flavor Crisco. Bake a few at a time for 12 to 15 minutes, or until deep golden brown, turning every 4 minutes. To serve, split with fork and toast. **About 2 dozen muffins**

Bismarcks →

1 package active dry yeast
¼ cup warm water (110° - 115°F)
⅓ cup Butter Flavor Crisco
1 cup milk
½ cup plus 3 tablespoons sugar
1 teaspoon salt
1 egg, slightly beaten
3½ to 4 cups all-purpose flour
    Butter Flavor Crisco for frying
¾ to 1 cup raspberry or grape jelly,
    or Vanilla Cream Filling, below

Vanilla Cream Filling (optional):
¼ cup sugar
2 tablespoons cornstarch
    Dash salt
¾ cup milk
1 egg yolk, beaten
2 tablespoons Butter Flavor Crisco
½ teaspoon vanilla

In large mixing bowl dissolve yeast in warm water. Set aside.

In small saucepan melt Butter Flavor Crisco. Stir in milk. Cool to 115°F.

Add 3 tablespoons sugar, salt and egg to yeast mixture. Stir in milk mixture. At low speed of electric mixer beat in flour, 1 cup at a time, until dough is stiff.

On well-floured board knead just until dough is no longer sticky. Place in greased bowl. Turn dough over. Cover; let rise in warm place until doubled, 1 to 1½ hours. Punch down dough. Continued as directed under photos below.

For Vanilla Cream Filling, in 1-quart saucepan combine sugar, cornstarch and salt. Stir in milk until smooth. Cook and stir over low heat until mixture thickens. Blend small amount of hot mixture into egg yolk. Blend back into hot mixture, stirring to combine. Cook and stir over low heat until mixture boils. Remove from heat. Stir in Butter Flavor Crisco and vanilla. Cool completely. (To prevent skin from forming, place small piece of plastic wrap directly on surface of thickened filling while cooling.) Pipe into cooled Bismarcks.

12 to 14 Bismarcks

How to Assemble Bismarcks

On floured board roll dough to ½-inch thickness. Cut into twelve to fourteen rounds with 3-inch floured cutter. Place on greased baking sheet.

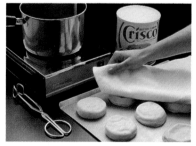

Cover; let rise in warm place until doubled, about 1 hour. In deep-fat fryer or deep saucepan heat 2 inches Butter Flavor Crisco to 350°F.

Fry a few at a time in hot oil for about 5 minutes, or until deep golden brown, turning once. Drain on paper towels.

Place remaining ½ cup sugar in large plastic bag. Shake one warm Bismarck at a time in bag to coat. Cool completely.

Make a small slit in each Bismarck by inserting a narrow knife blade through side to center.

Pipe about 1 tablespoon jelly or Vanilla Cream Filling through slit to center.

Buttermilk Doughnuts

3½ cups all-purpose flour, divided
¾ cup sugar
2 teaspoons baking powder
1 teaspoon baking soda
¾ teaspoon salt
1 teaspoon ground cinnamon
½ teaspoon ground nutmeg
¾ cup buttermilk
¼ cup Butter Flavor Crisco
2 eggs
1 teaspoon vanilla
  Butter Flavor Crisco for frying

Be sure to fry the holes, too. They'll disappear as fast as the doughnuts!

In large mixing bowl combine 2 cups flour, sugar, baking powder, baking soda, salt, cinnamon, nutmeg, buttermilk, Butter Flavor Crisco, eggs and vanilla. Beat at low speed of electric mixer until blended. Beat at medium speed for 2 minutes. Stir in remaining 1½ cups flour. Refrigerate for several hours or overnight.

Divide dough in half. Sprinkle lightly with flour. On well-floured board roll each half to slightly less than ½-inch thickness. Cut with floured 3-inch doughnut cutter.

In deep-fat fryer or deep saucepan heat 2 inches Butter Flavor Crisco to 375°F. Fry a few at a time in hot oil for 1 to 2 minutes on each side, or until golden brown. Drain on paper towels. Serve plain, dip tops in glazes (below), or shake cooled doughnuts in confectioners' sugar.

NOTE: Doughnut holes may be fried, cooled and coated with confectioners' sugar. Place doughnut holes in plastic bag. Add 2 to 4 tablespoons confectioners' sugar. Close bag and shake to coat.

Chocolate Doughnuts: Follow the recipe above, increasing flour to 3¾ cups. Increase sugar to 1 cup. Decrease baking powder to 1 teaspoon. Add 2 squares (1 ounce each) unsweetened chocolate, melted. Dip tops in Chocolate Glaze (below).

About 2 dozen doughnuts and holes

Glaze

1 cup confectioners' sugar
2 tablespoons hot water

In small bowl combine confectioners' sugar and hot water. Stir until smooth. Dip tops of doughnuts in glaze. Invert and place on wire rack until set.

Glazes 2 dozen doughnuts

Chocolate Glaze

2 tablespoons Butter Flavor Crisco
2 squares (1 ounce each) unsweetened chocolate
1 cup confectioners' sugar
¼ cup milk

In 1-quart saucepan melt Butter Flavor Crisco and chocolate over very low heat. Add confectioners' sugar and milk alternately, stirring until smooth. Dip tops of doughnuts in glaze. Invert and place on wire rack until set. **Glazes 2 dozen doughnuts**

Apple Fritters ✝

Butter Flavor Crisco for frying
1½ cups all-purpose flour
  3 tablespoons sugar
  2 tablespoons cornstarch
1½ teaspoons baking powder
 ½ teaspoon salt
 ¼ teaspoon ground allspice
 ¾ cup milk
  2 eggs, slightly beaten
  1 tablespoon Butter Flavor Crisco, melted
  2 cups chopped apples (about 2 medium)

In deep-fat fryer or deep saucepan heat 2 inches Butter Flavor Crisco to 375°F. In medium mixing bowl combine flour, sugar, cornstarch, baking powder, salt, allspice, milk, eggs and melted Butter Flavor Crisco. Stir with fork or wire whisk until just blended. Fold in apples.

Drop batter by level tablespoonfuls into hot oil. Fry a few at a time for 2 to 4 minutes, or until golden brown, turning 1 or 2 times. Drain on paper towels. Serve warm with maple syrup. Keep warm in single layer on paper towels in 175°F oven, if desired.

Corn Fritters: Follow the recipe above, omitting sugar, cornstarch and allspice. Substitute 1 cup canned or frozen whole kernel corn, thawed, for the apples. **About 4 dozen fritters**

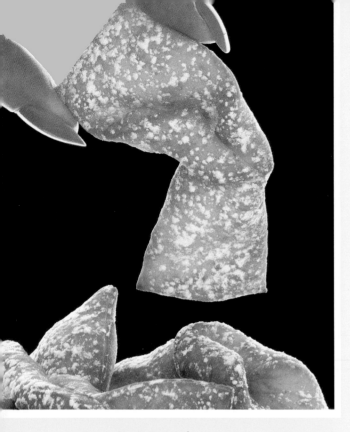

← Deep-Fried Bow Ties

¼ cup buttermilk
2 egg yolks
1 tablespoon sugar
1½ teaspoons vanilla
1½ teaspoons grated orange peel
¼ teaspoon salt
2 tablespoons Butter Flavor Crisco, melted
¾ cup plus 4 to 6 tablespoons all-purpose flour
Butter Flavor Crisco for frying
Confectioners' sugar

Prepare bow ties as directed below. In deep-fat fryer or deep saucepan heat about 2 inches Butter Flavor Crisco to 375°F. Fry several at a time for about 1½ minutes, or until golden brown, turning once. Drain on paper towels. Sift confectioners' sugar over both sides. Serve immediately or store in covered container.   **About 2 dozen bow ties**

How to Prepare Deep-Fried Bow Ties

In small mixing bowl combine buttermilk, egg yolks, sugar, vanilla, orange peel and salt. Slowly blend in melted Butter Flavor Crisco. Stir in ¾ cup flour.

Place dough on floured board. Knead in enough remaining flour to make soft dough that is easy to handle. On floured board, roll dough into a 12 × 12-inch square.

Cut into strips, about 4 × 1½ inches. Make 1-inch slit down the middle of each strip and pull one end through slit to make bow shape.

Zucchini Bread →

¾ cup sugar
½ cup Butter Flavor Crisco
1½ cups all-purpose flour
1 teaspoon baking soda
1 teaspoon ground cinnamon
½ teaspoon salt
¼ teaspoon ground nutmeg
⅛ teaspoon ground cloves
1 cup shredded zucchini
⅓ cup milk
2 eggs
½ cup chopped nuts

Preheat oven to 350°F. Grease 9 × 5 × 3-inch loaf pan on bottom only.

In medium mixing bowl cream sugar and Butter Flavor Crisco. Add flour, baking soda, cinnamon, salt, nutmeg, cloves, zucchini, milk, eggs and nuts. Beat at low speed of electric mixer until blended, scraping bowl frequently. Pour into prepared pan. Bake at 350°F for 45 to 50 minutes, or until wooden pick inserted in center comes out clean. Remove from pan. Cool on wire rack.

Carrot Bread: Follow the recipe above, substituting shredded carrot for the zucchini.

Banana Bread: Follow the recipe above, substituting 2 medium mashed bananas for the zucchini. Blend bananas with sugar and Butter Flavor Crisco. Decrease milk to 3 tablespoons and add 1 teaspoon lemon juice.

Apple Bread: Follow the recipe above, substituting 1 cup peeled, chopped apples for the zucchini.

1 loaf

Corn Bread ↑

1¼ cups milk
⅓ cup Butter Flavor Crisco, melted
2 eggs
1 cup all-purpose flour
1 cup yellow corn meal
2 tablespoons sugar
4 teaspoons baking powder
½ teaspoon salt

Preheat oven to 425°F. Grease 9 × 9 × 2-inch pan. Set aside.

In large mixing bowl blend milk, melted Butter Flavor Crisco and eggs. Add flour, corn meal, sugar, baking powder and salt. Stir only until dry ingredients are moistened. Pour into prepared pan.

Bake at 425°F for 20 to 25 minutes, or until golden brown. Serve warm.

Caraway and Cheese Corn Bread: Follow the recipe above, adding 1½ cups shredded Cheddar cheese and ½ teaspoon caraway seed with dry ingredients. **4 to 6 servings**

←**Corn Meal Muffins:** Follow the recipe above, increasing sugar to ¼ cup. Fill well-greased muffin cups ⅔ full. Bake at 425°F for 15 to 20 minutes, or until golden brown. *Pictured at left.* **12 muffins**

Blueberry Streusel Coffee Cake ⇢

Batter:
2⅓ cups all-purpose flour
1⅓ cups sugar
¾ teaspoon salt
¾ cup Butter Flavor Crisco
2 teaspoons baking powder
¾ cup milk
2 eggs
1 teaspoon vanilla

Filling:
1 cup ricotta cheese
1 egg
2 tablespoons sugar
1 tablespoon grated lemon peel
1 cup fresh or frozen blueberries,
    drained

Topping:
Reserved crumb mixture
½ cup chopped nuts
⅓ cup packed brown sugar
1 teaspoon ground cinnamon

Preheat oven to 350°F. Grease 13 × 9 × 2-inch pan. Set aside.

For batter, in large mixing bowl combine flour, sugar and salt. Cut in Butter Flavor Crisco until mixture is crumbly. Remove 1 cup mixture; set aside for topping. To remainder add baking powder, milk, eggs and vanilla. Beat on medium speed of electric mixer for 2 minutes, scraping bowl constantly. Pour into prepared pan. Set aside.

For filling, in medium bowl blend ricotta, egg, sugar and lemon peel until smooth. Sprinkle blueberries over batter in pan. Gently spread ricotta mixture over blueberries.

For topping, in small bowl mix reserved crumb mixture, nuts, brown sugar and cinnamon. Sprinkle over top of ricotta layer. Bake at 350°F for 45 to 60 minutes, or until wooden pick inserted in center comes out clean. Cool slightly before cutting.

Cranberry Streusel Coffee Cake: Follow the recipe above, substituting halved cranberries for blueberries and grated orange peel for lemon peel.

One 13 × 9-inch cake

105

Poppy Seed Muffins

2½ cups all-purpose flour
⅓ cup sugar
1 tablespoon plus 1 teaspoon baking powder
2 tablespoons poppy seed
1 teaspoon salt
1¼ cups milk
⅓ cup Butter Flavor Crisco, melted
2 eggs, beaten
1 teaspoon grated lemon peel

Preheat oven to 400°F. Line muffin cups with paper liners or grease well. Set aside.

In medium mixing bowl combine flour, sugar, baking powder, poppy seed and salt. Make well in center of mixture.

In small mixing bowl blend milk, melted Butter Flavor Crisco, eggs and lemon peel. Add to dry mixture. Stir only until dry ingredients are moistened. (Batter will be lumpy.) Fill prepared muffin cups about ⅔ full. Bake at 400°F for 20 to 25 minutes, or until golden brown.

Jam-Filled Muffins: Follow the recipe above, omitting poppy seed and lemon peel. Fill muffin cups ⅓ full. Top each with ½ teaspoon jam or jelly in center. Add remaining batter to fill each cup ⅔ full. Bake as directed.   **14 to 17 muffins**

Pineapple Bran Muffins

1 cup whole bran cereal
1 can (8 ounces) crushed pineapple (juice pack), undrained
½ cup milk
1 egg, beaten
¼ cup Butter Flavor Crisco, melted
1 cup all-purpose flour
½ cup sugar
⅓ cup chopped pecans
1 tablespoon baking powder
¼ teaspoon salt

Preheat oven to 400°F. Line muffin cups with paper liners or grease well. Set aside.

In small mixing bowl mix bran, pineapple and juice, milk and egg. Let stand for 3 minutes to soften bran. Stir in melted Butter Flavor Crisco.

In medium mixing bowl combine flour, sugar, pecans, baking powder and salt. Make well in center of mixture. Add bran mixture. Stir only until dry ingredients are moistened. Fill prepared muffin cups about ⅔ full. Bake at 400°F for 25 to 30 minutes, or until deep golden brown.

Honey Bran Muffins: Follow the recipe above, increasing milk to 1¼ cups. Omit pineapple and juice. Melt ¼ cup honey with Butter Flavor Crisco. Omit sugar and pecans.   **12 to 16 muffins**

Blueberry Muffins †

1¾ cups all-purpose flour
⅓ cup sugar
2 teaspoons baking powder
½ teaspoon salt
¾ cup milk
½ cup Butter Flavor Crisco, melted
1 egg, beaten
¾ cup frozen blueberries, thawed

Topping:
3 tablespoons sugar
¼ teaspoon ground cinnamon
¼ cup Butter Flavor Crisco, melted

Preheat oven to 400°F. Line muffin cups with paper liners or grease well. Set aside.

In medium mixing bowl combine flour, sugar, baking powder and salt. Make well in center of mixture. In small mixing bowl blend milk, melted Butter Flavor Crisco and egg. Add to dry mixture. Stir only until dry ingredients are moistened. (Batter will be lumpy.) Fold in blueberries. Fill prepared muffin cups about ⅔ full. Bake at 400°F for 15 to 20 minutes, or until golden brown. Remove from pan.

For topping, in small bowl mix sugar and cinnamon. While warm, dip tops of muffins in melted Butter Flavor Crisco and roll in sugar mixture to coat. **12 muffins**

107

← Waffles

   3 eggs, separated
1½ cups all-purpose flour
   2 tablespoons sugar or honey
   1 tablespoon baking powder
 ½ teaspoon salt
1¼ cups milk
 ⅓ cup Butter Flavor Crisco, melted

Heat waffle iron. In small mixing bowl beat egg whites until stiff. Set aside.

In medium mixing bowl combine flour, sugar, baking powder, salt, milk, melted Butter Flavor Crisco and egg yolks. Beat at lowest speed of electric mixer for 30 seconds. Fold in beaten egg whites.

Bake in hot waffle iron for 4 to 5 minutes, or until steaming stops and waffle is golden brown.

About seven 5-inch waffles

Buttery Cheese Biscuits
pictured on page 91

   2 cups all-purpose flour
   1 cup grated Cheddar cheese
   3 teaspoons baking powder
 ¾ teaspoon salt
 ½ cup Butter Flavor Crisco
 ⅔ to ¾ cup milk

Preheat oven to 425°F. In large mixing bowl combine flour, cheese, baking powder and salt. Cut in Butter Flavor Crisco to form coarse crumbs. Gradually add milk, mixing with fork until particles are moistened and cling together. Form dough into ball.

On floured board knead 8 to 10 times, or until dough is no longer sticky. Roll to ½-inch thickness. Cut with 2-inch floured biscuit cutter. Place on ungreased cookie sheet. Bake at 425°F for 10 to 15 minutes, or until lightly browned.

About 1 dozen biscuits

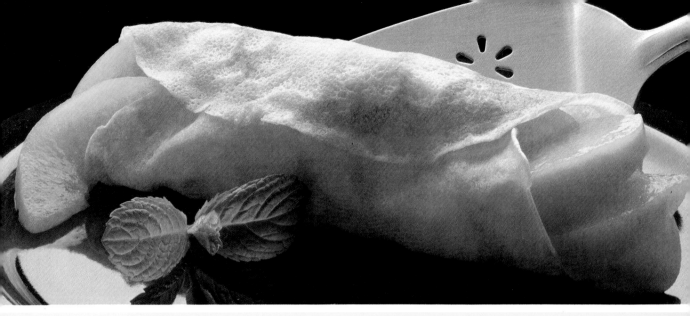

Crêpes ↑

　1　cup all-purpose flour
　¼　teaspoon salt
1¼　cups milk
　2　eggs
　2　tablespoons Butter Flavor Crisco,
　　　melted

In medium mixing bowl combine flour, salt, milk and eggs. Beat at medium speed of electric mixer until blended. Continue to beat at low speed, gradually adding melted Butter Flavor Crisco. Refrigerate for 1 hour.

Lightly grease non-stick 6-inch skillet with Butter Flavor Crisco. Heat pan over medium heat. Add 2 tablespoons batter. Immediately tilt and rotate skillet until batter forms a 6-inch crêpe. Cook for about 45 seconds to 1 minute, or until lightly browned. Turn with small spatula and brown other side for about 45 seconds. Cool on wire rack. Repeat with remaining batter to make about twenty crêpes.

TIP: Crêpes may be cooled, wrapped and refrigerated up to 2 days, or frozen.　**About 20 crêpes**

Dinner-Size Crêpes: Use 8-inch skillet and about 2½ tablespoons batter for each crêpe.　**12 crêpes**

Whole Wheat Pancakes

　1　egg, beaten
1¾　cups milk
　¼　cup Butter Flavor Crisco, melted
　¾　cup all-purpose flour
　¾　cup whole wheat flour
　2　tablespoons sugar
　1　tablespoon baking powder
　¾　teaspoon salt

Preheat griddle or electric fry pan to medium-high heat. In medium mixing bowl combine egg, milk, melted Butter Flavor Crisco, all-purpose flour, whole wheat flour, sugar, baking powder and salt. Beat with spoon just until dry ingredients are moistened.

Lightly grease heated griddle. A few drops of water sprinkled on griddle sizzle and bounce when heat is just right. Pour batter, about ¼ cup for each pancake, onto hot griddle. Bake until bubbles appear and edges are dry; turn and bake until other side is golden brown. Keep warm in 175°F oven on paper towel-lined baking sheet.
About twelve 5-inch pancakes

Buttermilk Pancakes: Follow the recipe above, substituting 2 cups buttermilk for the milk. Decrease baking powder to 2 teaspoons; add ½ teaspoon baking soda.　**About fifteen 5-inch pancakes**

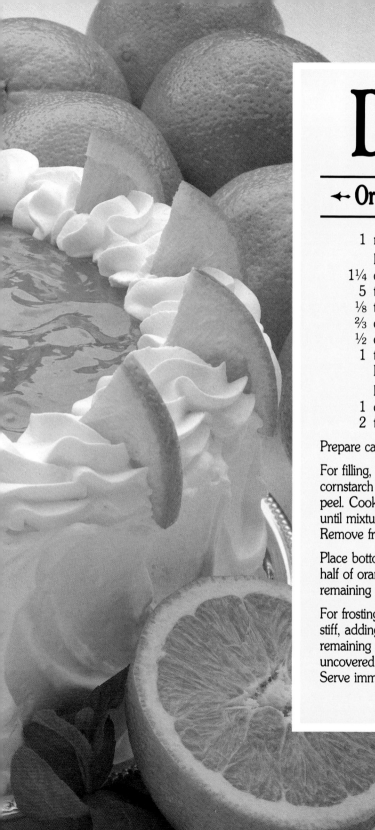

DESSERTS

← Orange-Filled Party Cake

  1 recipe Yellow Cake

Filling:
1¼ cups sugar
  5 tablespoons cornstarch
⅛ teaspoon salt
⅔ cup water
½ cup orange juice
  1 teaspoon grated orange peel
    Red and yellow food coloring (optional)

Frosting:
  1 cup whipping cream
  2 tablespoons sugar

Prepare cake in 2 layers as directed, page 114.

For filling, in small saucepan combine sugar, cornstarch and salt. Stir in water, orange juice and peel. Cook over medium heat, stirring constantly, until mixture thickens and becomes translucent. Remove from heat. Stir in food coloring. Cool.

Place bottom layer on serving plate. Spread with half of orange filling. Top with other layer. Spread remaining filling on top to within 1 inch of edge.

For frosting, in chilled mixing bowl whip cream until stiff, adding sugar gradually. Frost sides and remaining edge of top, leaving filling in center uncovered. Garnish with *orange slices,* if desired. Serve immediately or chill until served.

One 2-layer cake

CAKES

Butter Brickle Cake ← With Brown Sugar Glaze

¾ cup Butter Flavor Crisco
1⅔ cups sugar
3 eggs
2 teaspoons vanilla or rum extract
1 cup milk
2¾ cups all-purpose flour
1½ teaspoons baking powder
½ teaspoon salt
½ cup almond brickle chips

Glaze:
1 tablespoon packed brown sugar
½ cup confectioners' sugar
2½ to 3 teaspoons milk

Preheat oven to 350°F. Grease and flour 12-cup fluted ring pan. Set aside.

In large mixing bowl cream Butter Flavor Crisco, sugar, eggs and vanilla until light and fluffy. Add milk, flour, baking powder and salt. Beat at low speed of electric mixer until blended, scraping bowl constantly. Beat at medium speed for 2 minutes, scraping bowl occasionally. Stir in almond brickle chips. Pour into prepared pan.

Bake at 350°F for 55 to 60 minutes, or until wooden pick inserted in center comes out clean. Cool on wire rack for 15 minutes. Invert onto serving dish. Cool completely.

For glaze, in small bowl combine brown sugar and confectioners' sugar. Blend in milk until smooth and of desired consistency. Drizzle over cooled cake.

One ring cake

Jamaican Banana Cake With Broiled Topping ↑

⅔ cup Butter Flavor Crisco
1¼ cups sugar
1 teaspoon vanilla
2 eggs
1 cup milk
1 cup mashed bananas (about 2 medium)
2¼ cups all-purpose flour
1 teaspoon baking powder
1 teaspoon baking soda
½ teaspoon salt
½ cup chopped walnuts (optional)

Topping:
⅓ cup Butter Flavor Crisco
¾ cup packed brown sugar
2 tablespoons milk
1 cup flaked coconut
⅓ cup chopped walnuts

Preheat oven to 350°F. Grease and flour 13 × 9 × 2-inch pan. Set aside.

In large mixing bowl cream Butter Flavor Crisco, sugar, vanilla and eggs until light and fluffy. Add milk, bananas, flour, baking powder, baking soda and salt. Beat at low speed of electric mixer until blended, scraping bowl constantly. Beat at medium speed for 3 minutes, scraping bowl occasionally. Stir in walnuts. Pour into prepared pan.

Bake at 350°F for 40 to 45 minutes, or until golden brown and wooden pick inserted in center comes out clean. Cool for 5 minutes.

For topping, set oven to broil or 550°F. In small saucepan combine Butter Flavor Crisco, brown sugar and milk. Cook over medium heat, stirring constantly, for about 2 minutes, or until Butter Flavor Crisco melts. Stir in coconut and walnuts. Spread over warm cake. Broil 4 inches from heat for about 2 to 3 minutes, or until golden brown, watching carefully. Cool completely.

One 13 × 9-inch cake

113

Yellow Cake

⅔ cup Butter Flavor Crisco
2 cups sugar
3 eggs
1½ teaspoons vanilla
2¾ cups all-purpose flour
2½ teaspoons baking powder
½ teaspoon salt
1½ cups milk

Preheat oven to 350°F. Grease and flour 13 × 9 × 2-inch pan or two 9-inch round layer pans, or line cupcake pans. Set aside.

In large mixing bowl cream Butter Flavor Crisco, sugar, eggs and vanilla until light and fluffy. Add flour, baking powder, salt and milk. Beat at low speed of electric mixer until blended, scraping bowl constantly. Beat at medium speed for 2 minutes, scraping bowl occasionally. Pour into prepared pan(s).

Bake at 350°F, oblong or layers for 35 to 45 minutes, cupcakes for 25 to 30 minutes, or until center springs back when touched lightly. For layers, cool on wire rack for 5 minutes and remove from pans to cool completely. Frost as desired, page 128 or 129.

One 13 × 9-inch cake, two 9-inch layers, or 3 dozen cupcakes

Chocolate Cake

⅔ cup Butter Flavor Crisco
1⅔ cups sugar
2 eggs
1 teaspoon vanilla
1⅓ cups buttermilk
2 cups all-purpose flour
½ cup cocoa
1½ teaspoons baking soda
½ teaspoon baking powder
½ teaspoon salt

Preheat oven to 350°F. Grease and flour 13 × 9 × 2-inch pan or two 9-inch round layer pans, or line cupcake pans. Set aside.

In large mixing bowl cream Butter Flavor Crisco, sugar, eggs, and vanilla until light and fluffy. Add buttermilk, flour, cocoa, baking soda, baking powder and salt. Beat at low speed of electric mixer until blended, scraping bowl constantly. Beat at medium speed for 2 minutes, scraping bowl occasionally. Pour into prepared pan(s).

Bake at 350°F, oblong or layers for 35 to 45 minutes, cupcakes for 25 to 30 minutes, or until wooden pick inserted in center comes out clean. For layers, cool on wire rack for 5 minutes and remove from pans to cool completely. Frost as desired, page 128 or 129.

One 13 × 9-inch cake, two 9-inch layers, or 3 dozen cupcakes

Vanilla Cake
With Creamy Chocolate Frosting →

⅓ cup Butter Flavor Crisco
⅔ cup sugar
1 egg
¾ teaspoon vanilla
⅔ cup buttermilk
1⅓ cups all-purpose flour
½ teaspoon baking soda
½ teaspoon baking powder
¼ teaspoon salt

Frosting:
2 squares (1 ounce each) semi-sweet
   chocolate
1 tablespoon Butter Flavor Crisco
1⅓ cups confectioners' sugar
¼ teaspoon vanilla
1 tablespoon plus 1½ teaspoons
   to 2 tablespoons milk

Preheat oven to 350°F. Grease and flour
8 × 8 × 2-inch pan. Set aside.

In medium mixing bowl cream Butter Flavor Crisco,
sugar, egg and vanilla until light and fluffy. Add
buttermilk, flour, baking soda, baking powder and
salt. Beat at low speed of electric mixer until
blended, scraping bowl constantly. Beat at medium
speed for 1 minute, scraping bowl occasionally.
Pour into prepared pan.

Bake at 350°F for 35 to 45 minutes, or until
wooden pick inserted in center comes out clean.
Cool completely.

For frosting, in double boiler or saucepan over very
low heat melt chocolate, stirring constantly. Cool
slightly. Blend in Butter Flavor Crisco, confectioners'
sugar and vanilla. Add milk to desired consistency,
beating until smooth. Spread on cooled cake.

One 8 × 8-inch cake

115

Pistachio Pudding Cake
← With Pistachio Frosting

¾ cup Butter Flavor Crisco
1⅓ cups sugar
3 eggs
1 teaspoon vanilla
1¼ cups water
1 package (3¾ ounces) pistachio-
    flavored instant pudding mix
2¼ cups all-purpose flour
2 teaspoons baking powder

Frosting:
1 package (3¾ ounces) pistachio-
    flavored instant pudding mix
½ cup milk
1 container (8 ounces) prepared
    whipped topping (3½ cups), thawed
3 ounces pistachio nuts, shelled and
    finely chopped (about ⅓ cup)

Preheat oven to 350°F. Grease and flour two 9-inch
round layer pans. Set aside.

In large mixing bowl cream Butter Flavor Crisco,
sugar, eggs and vanilla until light and fluffy. Add
water, pudding mix, flour and baking powder. Beat
at low speed of electric mixer until blended,
scraping bowl constantly. Beat at medium speed for
2 minutes, scraping bowl occasionally. Pour into
prepared pans.

Bake at 350°F for 35 to 45 minutes, or until
wooden pick inserted in center comes out clean.
Cool for 5 minutes. Remove from pan. Cool
completely.

For frosting, in medium bowl combine pudding mix
and milk. Beat at medium speed for 1 minute. Fold
in whipped topping. Remove 1 cup frosting and
combine with chopped pistachio nuts. Spread on
bottom layer for filling. Top with other layer. Spread
remaining frosting on sides and top of cake. Chill
before serving.   **One 2-layer cake**

Applesauce Spice Cake ↑

⅔ cup Butter Flavor Crisco
1½ cups sugar
2 eggs
1 jar (15 ounces) applesauce
  (about 1½ cups)
2½ cups all-purpose flour
1½ teaspoons baking soda
½ teaspoon baking powder
½ teaspoon salt
½ teaspoon ground cinnamon
¼ teaspoon ground cloves
¼ teaspoon ground allspice
  Dash ground nutmeg
1 recipe Raisin Nut Frosting

Preheat oven to 350°F. Grease and flour two 9-inch round layer pans. Set aside.

In large mixing bowl cream Butter Flavor Crisco, sugar and eggs until light and fluffy. Add applesauce, flour, baking soda, baking powder, salt, cinnamon, cloves, allspice and nutmeg. Beat at low speed of electric mixer until blended, scraping bowl constantly. Beat at medium speed for 2 minutes, scraping bowl occasionally. Pour into prepared pans.

Bake at 350°F for 35 to 45 minutes, or until wooden pick inserted in center comes out clean. Cool on wire rack for 5 minutes. Remove from pans. Cool completely. Frost with Raisin Nut Frosting, page 128. **One 2-layer cake**

117

Oatmeal Cake
With Brown Sugar Frosting

¾ cup boiling water
⅔ cup rolled oats
⅓ cup Butter Flavor Crisco
⅔ cup packed dark brown sugar
⅓ cup granulated sugar
2 eggs
1 teaspoon maple flavoring
1⅓ cups all-purpose flour
¾ teaspoon baking soda
¼ teaspoon salt

Frosting:
1 tablespoon Butter Flavor Crisco
3 tablespoons packed dark brown sugar
3 tablespoons half-and-half
1 to 1½ cups confectioners' sugar

Preheat oven to 350°F. Grease and flour
9 × 9 × 2-inch pan. Set aside.

In small bowl combine boiling water and oats. Let
stand for 10 minutes.

Meanwhile, in medium mixing bowl cream Butter
Flavor Crisco, brown sugar, granulated sugar, eggs
and maple flavoring until light and fluffy. Add
oatmeal mixture, flour, baking soda and salt. Beat
at low speed of electric mixer until blended,
scraping bowl constantly. Beat at medium speed for
1 minute, scraping bowl occasionally. Pour into
prepared pan.

Bake at 350°F for 30 to 35 minutes, or until
wooden pick inserted in center comes out clean.
Cool completely.

For frosting, in small saucepan combine Butter
Flavor Crisco, brown sugar and half-and-half. Cook
over medium heat, stirring constantly, until mixture
boils. Remove from heat; cool to lukewarm. Beat in
powdered sugar to reach desired consistency.
Spread on cooled cake.   **One 9 × 9-inch cake**

Cranberry Orange Cake ↑

½ cup Butter Flavor Crisco
¾ cup packed brown sugar
2 eggs
1 jar (14 ounce) cranberry orange relish
¼ cup orange juice
1½ teaspoons grated orange peel
2½ cups all-purpose flour
1 teaspoon baking soda
½ cup chopped walnuts
1 recipe Orange Frosting

Preheat oven to 350°F. Grease and flour
13 × 9 × 2-inch pan. Set aside.

In large mixing bowl cream Butter Flavor Crisco,
brown sugar and eggs until light and fluffy. Add
cranberry-orange relish, orange juice and peel, flour
and baking soda. Beat at low speed of electric
mixer until blended, scraping bowl constantly. Beat
at medium speed for 2 minutes, scraping bowl
occasionally. Stir in walnuts. Pour into prepared
pan.

Bake at 350°F for 30 to 35 minutes, or until golden
brown and center springs back when touched
lightly. Cool completely. Frost with Orange Frosting,
page 129.   **One 13 × 9-inch cake**

Pound Cake

1½ cups Butter Flavor Crisco
 3 cups sugar
 5 eggs
 2 tablespoons lemon juice
 1 teaspoon vanilla
3¼ cups all-purpose flour
 1 teaspoon baking powder
 ½ teaspoon salt
1⅓ cups milk

Preheat oven to 350°F. Grease and flour 10-inch tube pan. Set aside.

In large mixing bowl combine Butter Flavor Crisco, sugar, eggs, lemon juice and vanilla. Beat at low speed of electric mixer until blended, scraping bowl constantly. Beat on high speed for 5 minutes, scraping bowl occasionally. In medium bowl combine flour, baking powder and salt. Mix in dry ingredients alternately with milk, beating after each addition until batter is smooth. Pour into prepared pan.

Bake at 350°F for 80 to 90 minutes, or until deep golden brown and wooden pick inserted in center comes out clean. Cool on wire rack for 20 minutes. Invert onto serving dish. Cool completely.

Caramel Pound Cake: Follow the recipe above, substituting 2 cups packed brown sugar and 1 cup granulated sugar for the 3 cups sugar. Substitute 1 teaspoon maple flavoring for the lemon juice and vanilla.

Chocolate Pound Cake: Follow the recipe above, increasing Butter Flavor Crisco to 1¾ cups. Omit lemon juice. Add ½ cup cocoa with flour.

One 10-inch tube cake

Chocolate-Chocolate Chip Cake ↑

 ½ cup Butter Flavor Crisco
 ⅔ cup sugar
 2 eggs
 ½ cup chocolate syrup
 ¼ cup dairy sour cream
 ½ teaspoon vanilla
 1 cup all-purpose flour
 ½ cup miniature chocolate chips
 ¾ teaspoon baking powder
 ¼ teaspoon salt
   Confectioners' sugar

Preheat oven to 350°F. Grease and flour 8 × 8 × 2-inch pan. Set aside.

In medium mixing bowl blend Butter Flavor Crisco, sugar, eggs, chocolate syrup, sour cream and vanilla. Add flour, chocolate chips, baking powder and salt. Beat at low speed of electric mixer until blended, scraping bowl constantly. Beat at medium speed for 1 minute, scraping bowl occasionally. Pour into prepared pan.

Bake at 350°F for 40 to 45 minutes, or until wooden pick inserted in center comes out clean. Cool completely. Sift confectioners' sugar over cake or frost as desired. **One 8 × 8-inch cake**

119

← Zucchini Cake

½ cup Butter Flavor Crisco
⅔ cup packed brown sugar
2 eggs
1 tablespoon molasses
½ cup buttermilk
1 cup shredded zucchini
1 cup all-purpose flour
1 teaspoon ground cinnamon
¾ teaspoon baking soda
¼ teaspoon salt

Preheat oven to 350°F. Grease and flour 8×8×2-inch pan. Set aside.

In large mixing bowl cream Butter Flavor Crisco, brown sugar, eggs and molasses until light and fluffy. Add buttermilk, zucchini, flour, cinnamon, baking soda and salt. Beat at low speed of electric mixer until blended, scraping bowl constantly. Beat at medium speed for 1 minute, scraping bowl occasionally. Pour into prepared pan.

Bake at 350°F for 30 to 35 minutes, or until center springs back when touched lightly. Cool on wire rack. Sift *confectioners' sugar* over cake using doily stencil, if desired.

One 8 × 8-inch cake

Butter Pecan Cake

⅔ cup Butter Flavor Crisco
½ cup packed brown sugar
1 cup granulated sugar
2 eggs
1 teaspoon vanilla
1 cup buttermilk
2 cups all-purpose flour
1½ teaspoons baking soda
½ teaspoon baking powder
½ teaspoon salt
½ cup chopped pecans
1 recipe Praline Frosting

Preheat oven to 350°F. Grease and flour 13×9×2-inch pan. Set aside.

In large mixing bowl cream Butter Flavor Crisco, brown sugar, granulated sugar, eggs and vanilla until light and fluffy. Add buttermilk, flour, baking soda, baking powder and salt. Beat at low speed of electric mixer until blended, scraping bowl constantly. Beat at medium speed for 2 minutes, scraping bowl occasionally. Stir in pecans. Pour into prepared pan.

Bake at 350°F for 35 to 40 minutes, or until wooden pick inserted in center comes out clean. Cool. Frost with Praline Frosting, page 129.

One 13 × 9-inch cake

Brandy Peach Cake With Brown Sugar Glaze →

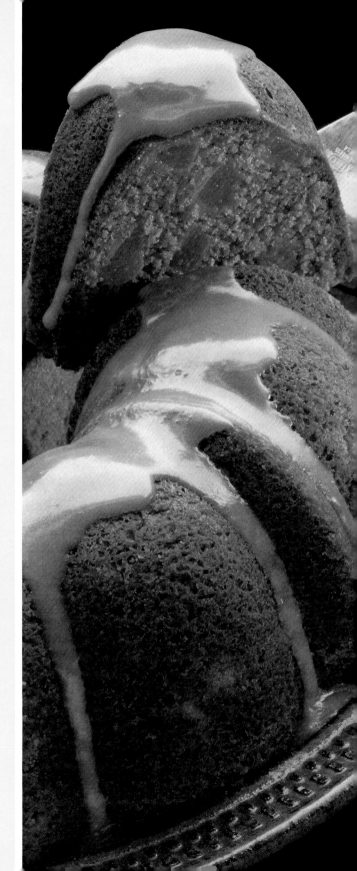

- 1 cup Butter Flavor Crisco
- 1 cup packed brown sugar
- 3 eggs
- 1 can (16 ounces) peach halves, drained and chopped
- ¾ cup milk
- 2 tablespoons brandy
- 2½ cups all-purpose flour
- 1 teaspoon ground cinnamon
- 1 teaspoon baking powder
- ½ teaspoon baking soda
- ½ teaspoon salt

Glaze:
- ½ cup confectioners' sugar
- 2 tablespoons packed brown sugar
- 3 to 4 teaspoons milk

Preheat oven to 350°F. Grease and flour 12-cup fluted ring pan. Set aside.

In large mixing bowl cream Butter Flavor Crisco, brown sugar and eggs. Add peaches, milk, brandy, flour, cinnamon, baking powder, baking soda and salt. Beat at low speed of electric mixer until blended, scraping bowl constantly. Beat at medium speed for 2 minutes, scraping bowl occasionally. Pour into prepared pan.

Bake at 350°F for 50 to 55 minutes, or until wooden pick inserted in center comes out clean and center springs back when touched lightly. Cool on wire rack for 5 minutes. Invert onto serving dish. Cool completely.

For glaze, in small mixing bowl comectioners' sugar and brown sugar. Stir in milk,
1 teaspoon at a time, until glaze is smooth and of desired consistency. Drizzle over cooled cake.

1 ring cake

Coconut Pineapple Upside-Down Cake ⬆

¼ cup Butter Flavor Crisco
½ cup packed brown sugar
1 can (8 ounces) crushed pineapple, drained, 2 tablespoons juice reserved
½ cup flaked coconut
1 cup all-purpose flour
¾ cup granulated sugar
½ cup milk
⅓ cup Butter Flavor Crisco
1 egg
1 teaspoon baking powder
¼ teaspoon salt

Preheat oven to 350°F. In 9-inch round layer pan blend ¼ cup Butter Flavor Crisco and brown sugar. Place in oven for 5 minutes to soften. Remove from oven. Add pineapple and coconut. Mix and spread in even layer over melted mixture in bottom of pan. Set aside.

In medium mixing bowl combine flour, sugar, milk, ⅓ cup Butter Flavor Crisco, egg, baking powder, salt and reserved pineapple juice. Beat at low speed of electric mixer until blended, scraping bowl constantly. Beat at medium speed for 1 minute, scraping bowl occasionally. Pour over pineapple mixture.

Bake at 350°F for 35 to 40 minutes, or until wooden pick inserted in center comes out clean. Invert on serving plate. Garnish with *maraschino cherries*, if desired. Serve warm or cool.

One 9-inch round cake

Pumpkin Cake With Spice Topping

½ cup Butter Flavor Crisco
¾ cup packed brown sugar
½ cup granulated sugar
3 eggs
1 can (16 ounces) pumpkin, ½ cup reserved
¼ cup milk
2½ cups all-purpose flour
1½ teaspoons baking soda
1½ teaspoons pumpkin pie spice
½ teaspoon baking powder
½ teaspoon salt

Topping:
Reserved pumpkin
2 tablespoons packed brown sugar
¼ teaspoon pumpkin pie spice
1 cup thawed prepared whipped topping

Preheat oven to 325°F. Grease and flour 13 × 9 × 2-inch pan. Set aside.

In large mixing bowl cream Butter Flavor Crisco, brown sugar, granulated sugar and eggs until light and fluffy. Add pumpkin (all but ½ cup), milk, flour, baking soda, pumpkin pie spice, baking powder and salt. Beat at low speed of electric mixer until blended, scraping bowl constantly. Beat at medium speed for 2 minutes, scraping bowl occasionally. Pour into prepared pan.

Bake at 325°F for 35 to 40 minutes, or until wooden pick inserted in center comes out clean and center springs back when touched lightly. Cool.

For topping, in small mixing bowl blend reserved pumpkin, brown sugar and pumpkin pie spice. Fold in whipped topping. Serve over cake.

One 13 × 9-inch cake

Rhubarb Cake With Spice Topping

½ cup Butter Flavor Crisco
¾ cup packed brown sugar
¼ cup granulated sugar
2 eggs
¾ teaspoon vanilla
½ cup milk
2 cups finely chopped rhubarb
1½ cups all-purpose flour
¾ teaspoon baking powder
½ teaspoon baking soda
¼ teaspoon salt
¼ teaspoon ground cinnamon
⅛ teaspoon ground nutmeg

Topping:
1 cup whipping cream
2 tablespoons granulated sugar
¼ teaspoon ground cinnamon
Dash nutmeg

Preheat oven to 350°F. Grease and flour 9 × 9 × 2-inch pan. Set aside.

In large mixing bowl cream Butter Flavor Crisco, brown sugar, granulated sugar, eggs and vanilla until light and fluffy. Add milk, rhubarb, flour, baking powder, baking soda, salt, cinnamon and nutmeg. Beat at low speed of electric mixer until blended, scraping bowl constantly. Beat at medium speed for 1 minute, scraping bowl occasionally. Pour into prepared pan.

Bake at 350°F for 45 to 55 minutes, or until wooden pick inserted in center comes out clean. Cool slightly.

For topping, in chilled mixing bowl beat whipping cream until thickened. Add sugar gradually, beating until stiff. Blend in cinnamon and nutmeg. Serve over warm cake. **One 9 × 9-inch cake**

Carrot Cake With Cream Cheese Glaze↑

¾ cup Butter Flavor Crisco
1½ cups sugar
3 eggs
¼ cup milk
2⅓ cups all-purpose flour
2 teaspoons baking soda
1 teaspoon ground cinnamon
½ teaspoon baking powder
½ teaspoon salt
2 cups grated carrots (about 4 medium)
⅔ cup raisins
½ cup chopped walnuts

Glaze:
1 ounce cream cheese, softened
½ cup confectoners' sugar
2 to 3 teaspoons milk

Preheat oven to 350°F. Grease and flour 12-cup fluted ring pan. Set aside.

In large mixing bowl cream Butter Flavor Crisco, sugar and eggs until light and fluffy. Add milk, flour, baking soda, cinnamon, baking powder and salt. Beat at low speed of electric mixer until blended, scraping bowl constantly. Beat at medium speed for 2 minutes, scraping bowl occasionally. Stir in carrots, raisins and walnuts. Pour into prepared pan.

Bake at 350°F for 50 to 55 minutes, or until wooden pick inserted in center comes out clean. Cool on wire rack for 5 minutes. Invert onto serving dish. Cool completely.

For glaze, in small dish combine cream cheese, confectioners' sugar and milk, beating until smooth and of desired consistency. Drizzle over cooled cake. **1 ring cake**

Sour Cream Raisin Cake With Raisin Topping↑

½ cup Butter Flavor Crisco
⅔ cup packed brown sugar
2 eggs
⅓ cup dairy sour cream
⅓ cup orange juice
1½ cups all-purpose flour
1 teaspoon baking soda
½ teaspoon baking powder
½ teaspoon salt
¼ teaspoon ground nutmeg
1 cup raisins

Topping:
¼ cup dairy sour cream
1 cup confectioners' sugar
¼ cup raisins

Preheat oven to 350°F. Grease and flour 9×9×2-inch pan. Set aside.

In large mixing bowl cream Butter Flavor Crisco, brown sugar, eggs and sour cream until light and fluffy. Add orange juice, flour, baking soda, baking powder, salt and nutmeg. Beat at low speed of electric mixer until blended, scraping bowl constantly. Beat at medium speed for 1 minute, scraping bowl occasionally. Stir in raisins. Pour into prepared pan.

Bake at 350°F for 35 to 40 minutes, or until wooden pick inserted in center comes out clean and center springs back when touched lightly. Cool completely.

For topping, in small bowl combine sour cream and confectioners' sugar. Beat until smooth. Stir in raisins. Spread on cooled cake.

One 9×9-inch cake

Cherry Cake With Almond Glaze ↑

⅔ cup Butter Flavor Crisco
1⅔ cups sugar
3 eggs
1 jar (10 ounces) maraschino cherries,
  drained (⅓ cup juice reserved),
  and chopped
1 cup milk
3 cups all-purpose flour
2 teaspoons baking powder

Glaze:
½ cup confectioners' sugar
1½ to 2½ teaspoons milk
¼ teaspoon almond extract

Preheat oven to 350°F. Grease and flour 12-cup fluted ring pan. Set aside.

In large mixing bowl cream Butter Flavor Crisco, sugar and eggs until light and fluffy. Add cherries, reserved cherry juice, milk, flour and baking powder. Beat at low speed of electric mixer until blended, scraping bowl constantly. Beat at medium speed for 2 minutes, scraping bowl occasionally. Pour into prepared pan.

Bake at 350°F for 50 to 60 minutes, or until wooden pick inserted in center comes out clean and center springs back when touched lightly. Cool on wire rack for 5 minutes. Invert onto serving dish. Cool completely.

For glaze, in small bowl blend confectioners' sugar, milk and almond extract until smooth and of desired consistency. Drizzle over cooled cake.

1 ring cake

Orange Yogurt Cake

2/3 cup Butter Flavor Crisco
1½ cups sugar
3 eggs
1 cup (8 ounces) plain yogurt
½ cup orange juice
2 teaspoons grated orange peel
2⅔ cups all-purpose flour
1½ teaspoons baking soda
½ teaspoon baking powder
¼ teaspoon salt
1 recipe Buttery Cream Frosting

Preheat oven to 350°F. Grease and flour two 9-inch round layer pans. Set aside.

In large mixing bowl cream Butter Flavor Crisco, sugar and eggs until light and fluffy. Add yogurt, orange juice and peel, flour, baking soda, baking powder and salt. Beat at low speed of electric mixer until blended, scraping bowl constantly. Beat at medium speed for 2 minutes, scraping bowl occasionally. Pour into prepared pans. Bake at 350°F for 35 to 40 minutes, or until golden brown and center springs back when touched lightly. Cool for 5 minutes. Remove from pan. Cool completely. Frost with Buttery Cream Frosting, page 128.

Two 9-inch layers

Red Velvet Cake ✝

2/3 cup Butter Flavor Crisco
1¾ cups sugar
2 eggs
1 teaspoon vanilla
2 tablespoons cocoa
2 tablespoons (1 ounce) red food coloring
1 cup buttermilk
2⅓ cups all-purpose flour
1 teaspoon baking soda
½ teaspoon salt
1 recipe Fluffy Frosting

Preheat oven to 350°F. Grease and flour two 9-inch round layer pans. Set aside.

In large mixing bowl cream Butter Flavor Crisco, sugar, eggs and vanilla until light and fluffy. In 1-cup measure combine cocoa and food coloring, stirring until smooth. Blend into creamed mixture. Add buttermilk, flour, baking soda and salt. Beat at low speed of electric mixer until blended, scraping bowl constantly. Beat at medium speed for 2 minutes, scraping bowl occasionally. Pour into prepared pans.

Bake at 350°F for 35 to 40 minutes, or until center springs back when touched lightly. Cool for 5 minutes. Remove from pan. Cool completely. Frost with Fluffy Frosting, page 128.   **Two 9-inch layers**

← Fluffy Frosting

¼ cup all-purpose flour
1 cup milk
¾ cup Butter Flavor Crisco
1¼ cups sugar
1 teaspoon vanilla

In small saucepan combine flour and milk. Cook over medium heat, stirring constantly. Heat to boiling; cook, stirring constantly, for 5 to 8 minutes, or until *very* thick. Cool completely.

In medium bowl combine Butter Flavor Crisco, sugar and vanilla. Add thickened mixture. Beat on high speed of electric mixer for about 5 minutes, or until smooth and creamy. Spread on cooled cake.

Fills and frosts two 8- or 9-inch layers

← Raisin Nut Frosting

⅔ cup Butter Flavor Crisco
1 package (8 ounces) cream cheese, softened
½ teaspoon vanilla
4 cups confectioners' sugar
Half-and-half or milk
⅓ cup raisins
⅓ cup chopped walnuts

In medium mixing bowl combine Butter Flavor Crisco, cream cheese and vanilla. Add confectioners' sugar, beating until blended. If needed, add 1 to 2 teaspoons half-and-half or milk to reach desired consistency. Stir in raisins and walnuts. Spread on cooled cake.

Fills and frosts two 8- or 9-inch layers

↑ Buttery Cream Frosting

4 cups confectioners' sugar
⅓ cup Butter Flavor Crisco
1½ teaspoons vanilla
6 to 7 tablespoons milk

In medium mixing bowl combine confectioners' sugar, Butter Flavor Crisco and vanilla. Slowly blend in milk to desired consistency. Beat on high speed for 5 minutes, or until smooth and creamy.

Fills and frosts two 8- or 9-inch layers or
frosts one 13 × 9-inch cake

Chocolate Frosting ➠

3 cups confectioners' sugar, divided
⅓ cup cocoa
½ cup Butter Flavor Crisco
½ teaspoon vanilla
5 to 6 tablespoons half-and-half or milk, divided

In medium mixing bowl combine 2 cups confectioners' sugar and cocoa. Add Butter Flavor Crisco and vanilla. Blend at low speed of electric mixer. Blend in 2 tablespoons half and half. Beat in remaining sugar. Blend in remaining half-and-half until frosting is smooth and of desired consistency.

Mocha Frosting: Follow the recipe above, substituting 1 teaspoon instant coffee dissolved in 1 tablespoon hot water for 1 tablespoon of half-and-half.

Fills and frosts two 8- or 9-inch round layers or frosts one 13 × 9-inch cake

Praline Frosting ➠

¼ cup Butter Flavor Crisco
½ cup chopped pecans
¼ cup milk
½ teaspoon vanilla
3 to 3½ cups confectioners' sugar

In small saucepan combine Butter Flavor Crisco and pecans. Cook over medium heat until Butter Flavor Crisco melts. Remove from heat. Blend in milk and vanilla. Transfer to medium mixing bowl. Add confectioners' sugar, 1 cup at a time, beating at medium speed of electric mixer until frosting is of desired consistency. Spread on cooled cake.

Frosts one 13 × 9-inch cake

Orange Frosting ↑

3 cups confectioners' sugar
3 tablespoons Butter Flavor Crisco
½ teaspoon grated orange peel
⅓ cup orange juice

In medium mixing bowl combine confectioners' sugar, Butter Flavor Crisco and orange peel. Gradually add orange juice, beating until smooth and of desired consistency. Spread on cooled cake.

Frosts one 13 × 9-inch cake

COOKIES

← Basic Sugar Cookies

  1 cup Butter Flavor Crisco
  1 cup sugar
  1 egg
  ½ teaspoon vanilla or ¼ teaspoon
     almond extract
2¼ cups all-purpose flour
  1 teaspoon baking powder
  ¼ teaspoon salt

In large mixing bowl cream Butter Flavor Crisco, sugar, egg and vanilla until light and fluffy. Mix in flour, baking powder and salt. Divide dough in half and form into 2 balls. Cover and refrigerate for at least 2 hours.

Preheat oven to 375°F. Roll dough ¼ to ⅛ inch thick on lightly floured board. Cut shapes with 2- or 2½-inch cookie cutter. Place 1 inch apart on ungreased baking sheet. Bake at 375°F for 7 to 9 minutes, or until light golden brown around edges. Remove to cooling rack.

Lemon Sugar Cookies: Follow the recipe above, substituting ¼ teaspoon lemon extract for the vanilla. Add 1 teaspoon grated lemon peel to creamed mixture. **4 to 4½ dozen cookies**

Jam-Filled Sugar Cookies

  1 recipe Basic Sugar Cookies
  ¼ cup jam (any flavor)
     Confectioners' sugar

Prepare and refrigerate dough as directed above. Preheat oven to 375°F. Roll dough ⅛ inch thick on lightly floured board. Cut shapes with 2-inch round cookie cutter. Place one cutout on ungreased baking sheet. Spread ¼ teaspoon jam on center of cutout, leaving ¼ inch around edge. Place another cutout on top. Press edges together to seal. Repeat for remaining cookies, placing 1 inch apart. Bake at 375°F for 8 to 10 minutes, or until edges are light golden brown. Remove to cooling rack. Cool for 5 minutes; sift confectioners' sugar over cookies.
3½ to 4 dozen cookies

Surprise Sugar Cookies

1 recipe Basic Sugar Cookies
4 to 4½ dozen (about 2½ ounces) whole
    blanched skinned almonds or 4 to 4½
    dozen (about 10 ounces) whole
    maraschino cherries, well drained

Prepare dough as directed at left. Cover and
refrigerate for 30 minutes. Preheat oven to 350°F.
Wrap about 1 tablespoon dough around each
whole almond or cherry. Roll into smooth ball.
Place 2 inches apart on ungreased baking sheet.
Bake at 350°F for 12 to 15 minutes, or until light
golden brown. Remove to cooling rack.

4 to 4½ dozen cookies

Chocolate Mint Cookies

1 cup semi-sweet chocolate chips
½ cup Butter Flavor Crisco
⅓ cup packed brown sugar
⅓ cup granulated sugar
1 egg
¼ teaspoon peppermint extract
1½ cups all-purpose flour
½ teaspoon baking soda
¼ teaspoon salt

Preheat oven to 350°F. In double boiler or small
saucepan over very low heat, melt chocolate chips.
Set aside to cool.

In large mixing bowl cream Butter Flavor Crisco,
brown sugar, granulated sugar and egg. Blend in
peppermint extract and melted chocolate. Add
flour, baking soda and salt; mix well. Shape dough
by rounded teaspoonfuls into balls. Place 2 inches
apart on ungreased baking sheet. Flatten in
crisscross pattern with tines of fork.

Bake at 350°F for 10 to 12 minutes, or until set.
Remove to cooling rack. Sift *confectioners' sugar*
over cookies, if desired.   **3 to 3½ dozen cookies**

Fudge Cake Cookies ↑

1 cup Butter Flavor Crisco
1 cup sugar
½ cup cocoa
2 eggs
½ cup buttermilk
3 cups all-purpose flour
½ teaspoon baking soda
½ teaspoon salt
1 recipe Chocolate Cookie Frosting

In large mixing bowl blend Butter Flavor Crisco,
sugar, cocoa, eggs and buttermilk. Mix in flour,
baking soda and salt. Cover and refrigerate dough
for at least 3 hours.

Preheat oven to 350°F. Shape dough into 1-inch
balls. Place 2 inches apart on ungreased baking
sheet. Bake at 350°F for 10 to 12 minutes, or until
set. Remove to cooling rack. Frost with Chocolate
Cookie Frosting, page 140. Store in covered
container.   **5 to 5½ dozen cookies**

131

Brown Sugar Cookies

1 cup Butter Flavor Crisco
1 cup packed brown sugar
1 egg
1 teaspoon vanilla
2 cups all-purpose flour
½ teaspoon baking soda
¼ teaspoon salt

Preheat oven to 350°F. In large mixing bowl cream Butter Flavor Crisco and brown sugar, egg and vanilla until light and fluffy. Mix in flour, baking soda and salt. Shape dough into 1-inch balls. Place 2 inches apart on ungreased baking sheet. Bake at 350°F for 12 to 14 minutes, or until golden brown. Remove to cooling rack after 1 minute.

4 to 4½ dozen cookies

Variations: *(pictured, top to bottom)*

Coconut Cookies: Follow the recipe above, adding 1½ cups flaked coconut. Shape and bake as directed. **4½ to 5 dozen cookies**

Peanut Cookies: Follow the recipe above, omitting salt. Stir in 1 package (6 ounces) semi-sweet chocolate chips and 1 cup chopped salted peanuts after adding dry ingredients. Drop by rounded teaspoonfuls 2 inches apart onto ungreased baking sheet. Bake as directed. **5 to 5½ dozen cookies**

Cinnamon Molasses Cookies: Follow the recipe above, adding 1 tablespoon molasses to creamed mixture. Add 2 teaspoons ground cinnamon with dry ingredients. Shape as directed. Flatten with bottom of glass dipped in granulated sugar. Bake at 350°F for 8 to 10 minutes, or until light golden brown. Remove to cooling rack after 1 minute.

4½ to 5 dozen cookies

Carrot Cookies: Follow the recipe above, adding 1 jar (7½ ounces) carrot baby food to creamed mixture. Add ¼ teaspoon ground ginger, ¼ teaspoon ground allspice and ¼ teaspoon ground nutmeg with dry ingredients. Drop by rounded teaspoonfuls 2 inches apart onto lightly greased baking sheet. Bake at 350°F for 10 to 12 minutes, or until set. Remove immediately to cooling rack. When cool, frost with Cream Cheese Frosting (below). **4½ to 5 dozen cookies**

↑ Cream Cheese Frosting

1 package (3 ounces) cream cheese
2 tablespoons Butter Flavor Crisco
1½ cups confectioners' sugar
1 teaspoon milk

In medium mixing bowl blend cream cheese and Butter Flavor Crisco. Mix in confectioners' sugar. Add milk and beat until smooth and creamy.

Frosts 4½ to 5 dozen cookies

Spritz ↑

1 cup Butter Flavor Crisco
2/3 cup sugar
1 egg
1 teaspoon vanilla
5 to 6 drops food coloring, optional
1¾ cups all-purpose flour
¼ teaspoon salt

In large mixing bowl cream Butter Flavor Crisco, sugar, egg and vanilla until light and fluffy. Stir in food coloring. Add flour and salt in four parts, mixing well after each addition. Cover and refrigerate dough for 1 hour.

Preheat oven to 375°F. Place dough in cookie press. Press into desired shapes on ungreased baking sheet. Bake at 375°F for 8 to 10 minutes, or until edge is light golden brown. Remove to cooling rack.

Almond or Lemon Spritz: Follow the recipe above, substituting ¼ teaspoon almond or lemon extract for the vanilla. **5 to 6 dozen cookies**

Oatmeal Crispies

1 cup Butter Flavor Crisco
½ cup granulated sugar
½ cup packed brown sugar
1 egg
1 teaspoon vanilla
1¼ cups all-purpose flour
½ teaspoon baking soda
¼ teaspoon salt
¼ teaspoon ground nutmeg
¼ teaspoon ground cinnamon
1½ cups rolled oats
½ cup chopped nuts
½ cup raisins

Preheat oven to 375°F. In large mixing bowl cream Butter Flavor Crisco, granulated sugar, brown sugar, egg and vanilla until light and fluffy. Mix in flour, baking soda, salt, nutmeg and cinnamon. Stir in rolled oats, nuts and raisins.

Drop by rounded teaspoonfuls 2 inches apart on ungreased baking sheet. Bake at 375°F for 11 to 14 minutes, or until golden brown. Remove to cooling rack after 1 minute. **4 to 4½ dozen cookies**

Molasses Cookies ↑

⅓ cup Butter Flavor Crisco
½ cup sugar
1 egg
⅓ cup molasses
2¼ cups all-purpose flour
1 teaspoon baking soda
½ teaspoon ground cinnamon
1½ teaspoons ground ginger
¼ teaspoon ground nutmeg
¼ teaspoon ground cloves
¼ teaspoon salt
   Sugar

In large mixing bowl cream Butter Flavor Crisco, sugar, egg and molasses until light and fluffy. Mix in flour, baking soda, cinnamon, ginger, nutmeg, cloves and salt. Cover and refrigerate for 1 hour.

Preheat oven to 375°F. Grease baking sheets. Set aside.

Shape into 1-inch balls. Roll in sugar. Place 2 inches apart on prepared baking sheet. Flatten each cookie with bottom of drinking glass. Bake at 375°F for about 10 minutes. Remove to cooling rack.

3½ to 4 dozen cookies

Swedish Spice Cookies ↑

½ cup Butter Flavor Crisco
¾ cup sugar
1 egg
¼ cup dairy sour cream
2 teaspoons dried grated orange peel
1 teaspoon ground cardamom
¼ teaspoon ground ginger
¼ teaspoon ground cloves
2⅓ cups all-purpose flour
½ teaspoon baking soda
   Sugar

Preheat oven to 350°F. Grease baking sheets. Set aside.

In large mixing bowl cream Butter Flavor Crisco and sugar until light and fluffy. Blend in egg and sour cream. Stir in orange peel, cardamom, ginger and cloves. Mix in flour and baking soda.

Shape dough into 1-inch balls. Roll in sugar. Place 2 inches apart on prepared baking sheet. Flatten each cookie with bottom of drinking glass. Bake at 350°F for 8 to 10 minutes, or until light golden brown. Remove to cooling rack.

5 to 5½ dozen cookies

Granola Cookies ↑

1¼ cups Butter Flavor Crisco
1 cup granulated sugar
⅔ cup packed brown sugar
¼ cup honey
2 eggs
1 teaspoon vanilla
2½ cups all-purpose flour
1 teaspoon baking soda
½ teaspoon salt
1 cup rolled oats
1 cup flaked coconut
1 cup raisins
½ cup wheat germ
½ cup chopped nuts

Preheat oven to 350°F. In large mixing bowl cream Butter Flavor Crisco, granulated sugar, brown sugar, honey, eggs and vanilla until light and fluffy. Mix in flour, baking soda and salt. Stir in rolled oats, coconut, raisins, wheat germ and nuts.

Drop by rounded teaspoonfuls 2 inches apart onto ungreased baking sheet. Bake at 350°F for 14 to 17 minutes, or until golden brown. Remove to cooling rack. **5 to 5½ dozen cookies**

Mexican Wedding Cakes ↑

1⅓ cups Butter Flavor Crisco
⅔ cup confectioners' sugar
½ teaspoon vanilla
2¼ cups all-purpose flour
⅛ teaspoon salt
1 cup finely chopped pecans
Confectioners' sugar

In large mixing bowl cream Butter Flavor Crisco, confectioners' sugar and vanilla until light and fluffy. Add flour, salt and pecans; mix well. Cover and refrigerate for at least 2 hours.

Preheat oven to 325°F. Shape dough into 1- to 1½-inch balls. Place 2 inches apart on ungreased baking sheet. Bake at 325°F for about 25 minutes, or until bottom edges of cookies are light brown. Roll warm cookies in confectioners' sugar. Remove to cooling rack. **2½ to 3½ dozen cookies**

135

Slice & Bake
Coffee Spice Cookies →

1 teaspoon instant coffee
1 teaspoon hot water
½ cup Butter Flavor Crisco
¾ cup packed brown sugar
1 egg
½ teaspoon vanilla
1½ cups all-purpose flour
1 teaspoon baking powder
½ teaspoon ground cinnamon
¼ teaspoon ground nutmeg
¼ teaspoon salt
⅓ cup chocolate jimmies

In measuring cup dissolve instant coffee in hot water. In large mixing bowl cream Butter Flavor Crisco, brown sugar, egg, vanilla and coffee mixture until light and fluffy. Mix in flour, baking powder, cinnamon, nutmeg and salt.

Divide dough into two equal parts. Shape each part into roll 1½ inches in diameter and about 7 inches long. Roll in chocolate jimmies, pressing lightly. Wrap; refrigerate for at least 2 hours.

Preheat oven to 375°F. Cut rolls into ¼-inch slices. Place slices 1 inch apart on ungreased baking sheet. Bake at 375°F for 6 to 8 minutes, or until set. Remove to cooling rack.   **5 to 5½ dozen cookies**

Slice & Bake
Chocolate Cookies →

½ cup Butter Flavor Crisco
2 ounces unsweetened chocolate, melted
1 cup sugar
1 egg
½ teaspoon vanilla
1¼ cups all-purpose flour
1 teaspoon baking powder
¼ teaspoon salt
⅓ cup finely chopped pecans

In large mixing bowl blend Butter Flavor Crisco and melted chocolate. Blend in sugar, egg and vanilla. Mix in flour, baking powder and salt. Divide dough into two equal parts. Shape each part into a roll 1½ inches in diameter and about 7 inches long. Roll in pecans to coat, pressing lightly. Wrap; refrigerate for at least 2 hours.

Preheat oven to 375°F. Cut rolls into ¼-inch slices. Place slices 1 inch apart on ungreased baking sheet. Bake at 375°F for 8 to 10 minutes, or until set. Remove to cooling rack.   **4½ to 5 dozen cookies**

Slice & Bake Peanut Butter Cookies →

½ cup Butter Flavor Crisco
½ cup creamy peanut butter
¾ cup granulated sugar
½ cup packed brown sugar
2 eggs
1 teaspoon vanilla
2½ cups all-purpose flour
1 teaspooon baking soda
1 teaspoon baking powder
½ teaspoon salt
¾ cup finely chopped peanuts

In large mixing bowl cream Butter Flavor Crisco, peanut butter, granulated sugar, brown sugar, eggs and vanilla until light and fluffy. Mix in flour, baking soda, baking powder and salt. Divide dough into three equal parts. Shape each part into a roll 1½ inches in diameter and about 7 inches long. Roll in finely chopped peanuts, pressing lightly. Wrap; refrigerate for at least 3 hours.

Preheat oven to 375°F. Cut rolls into ¼-inch slices. Place slices 1 inch apart on ungreased baking sheet. Bake at 375°F for 7 to 9 minutes, or until set. Remove to cooling rack.   **6½ to 7 dozen cookies**

Peanut Butter Chip Cookies

½ cup Butter Flavor Crisco
⅓ cup peanut butter
1 cup packed brown sugar
½ cup granulated sugar
2 eggs
1 teaspoon vanilla
1¾ cups all-purpose flour
¾ teaspoon baking soda
¼ teaspoon salt
1 package (6 ounces) peanut butter flavored chips or semi-sweet chocolate chips

Preheat oven to 375°F. In large mixing bowl cream Butter Flavor Crisco, peanut butter, brown sugar, granulated sugar, eggs and vanilla until light and fluffy. Mix in flour, baking soda and salt. Stir in peanut butter chips.

Drop by rounded teaspoonfuls 2 inches apart onto ungreased baking sheet. Bake at 375°F for 10 to 12 minutes, or until golden brown. Remove to cooling rack. **4½ to 5 dozen cookies**

✦ Fruitcake Cookies

1 pound dried fruitcake mix (2¾ cups)
2 tablespoons brandy or orange juice
1 cup Butter Flavor Crisco
¾ cup packed dark brown sugar
¼ cup molasses
2 eggs
¾ teaspoon ground cinnamon
¼ teaspoon ground nutmeg
1¾ cups all-purpose flour
½ teaspoon baking powder
½ teaspoon baking soda
1 cup chopped walnuts

Preheat oven to 350°F. Grease baking sheets. Set aside.

Place fruitcake mix in small mixing bowl. Sprinkle with brandy. Set aside.

In large mixing bowl cream Butter Flavor Crisco, brown sugar, molasses, eggs, cinnamon and nutmeg until light and fluffy. Mix in flour, baking powder and baking soda. Stir in fruit mixture and walnuts.

Drop by rounded teaspoonfuls 2 inches apart onto prepared baking sheet. Bake at 350°F for 11 to 13 minutes, or until set. Remove to cooling rack after 1 minute. **5 to 5½ dozen cookies**

Cappuccino Cookies

1 teaspoon instant coffee
1 tablespoon hot water
¾ cup Butter Flavor Crisco
1 cup sugar
1 egg
¼ cup orange juice
1 tablespoon grated orange peel
2¼ cups all-purpose flour
½ teaspoon soda
¼ teaspoon salt

Preheat oven to 350°F. Grease baking sheets. Set aside.

In small dish dissolve instant coffee in hot water. In large mixing bowl cream Butter Flavor Crisco, sugar, egg, orange juice and peel and coffee mixture until light and fluffy. Mix in flour, baking soda and salt. Drop by rounded teaspoonfuls 2 inches apart onto prepared baking sheet. Bake at 350°F for 13 to 16 minutes, or until set. Remove to cooling rack. Frost with *Basic Cookie Frosting*, page 140, if desired.   **2½ to 3 dozen cookies**

Flaky Wafer Cookies†

2 cups all-purpose flour
¼ cup confectioners' sugar
¼ teaspoon salt
⅔ cup Butter Flavor Crisco
3 to 4 tablespoons half-and-half
2 egg yolks
1 teaspoon vanilla
1 recipe Basic Cookie Frosting

In large mixing bowl combine flour, confectioners' sugar and salt. With fork or pastry blender cut in Butter Flavor Crisco to form fine particles. In small bowl combine 3 tablespoons half-and-half, egg yolks and vanilla. Sprinkle over flour mixture, mixing until particles are moistened. If needed, add additional tablespoon half-and-half. Form dough into 2 balls. Wrap each in plastic wrap and refrigerate for at least 1 hour.

Preheat oven to 400°F. Roll dough ¼ inch thick on lightly floured board. Cut into 1½- to 2-inch shapes. Prick cutouts with fork. Place on ungreased baking sheet. Bake at 400°F for 8 to 10 minutes, or until edge is light golden brown. Remove to cooling rack. Frost with *Basic Cookie Frosting*, page 140.
2½ to 3 dozen cookies

← Brownies

1 cup Butter Flavor Crisco
1½ cups sugar
2 eggs
1 teaspoon vanilla
⅔ cup milk
1 cup all-purpose flour
½ cup cocoa
1 teaspoon baking powder
¼ teaspoon salt
½ cup chopped walnuts

Preheat oven to 350°F. Grease 13×9×2-inch pan. Set aside.

In medium mixing bowl cream Butter Flavor Crisco, sugar, eggs and vanilla until light and fluffy. Add milk, flour, cocoa, baking powder and salt. Beat at low speed of electric mixer until blended. Beat at high speed for 1 minute. Stir in nuts. Pour into prepared pan.

Bake at 350°F for 30 to 35 minutes, or until a wooden pick inserted in center comes out clean. Cool. Frost, if desired. Cut into bars, about 2 × 1½ inches. **32 bars**

Basic Cookie Frosting

3 tablespoons Butter Flavor Crisco
1¼ cups confectioners' sugar
1 teaspoon vanilla
Dash salt
2½ to 3½ teaspoons half-and-half or milk
1 to 2 drops food coloring (optional)

In small mixing bowl blend Butter Flavor Crisco, confectioners' sugar, vanilla and salt. Blend in half-and-half to desired consistency. Beat until smooth. Blend in food coloring. Spread on cooled cookies. **⅔ cup frosting**

Chocolate Cookie Frosting: Follow the recipe above, adding 2 tablespoons cocoa with the confectioners' sugar. Increase half-and-half to 1 tablespoon plus 1½ to 2½ teaspoons.

¾ cup frosting

Coffee Orange Cookie Frosting

½ teaspoon instant coffee
1 tablespoon hot water
3 tablespoons Butter Flavor Crisco
1¼ cups confectioners' sugar
½ teaspoon grated orange peel
Dash salt
1 to 2 teaspoons water

Dissolve coffee in hot water. Set aside. In small mixing bowl blend Butter Flavor Crisco, confectioners' sugar, orange peel and salt. Add coffee mixture and beat until smooth. If necessary, add 1 to 2 teaspoons water until frosting reaches desired consistency. Spread on cooled cookies.

¾ cup frosting

Layered Fruit Bars ➙

1 cup Butter Flavor Crisco
1 cup packed brown sugar
½ teaspoon vanilla
2 cups all-purpose flour
　Dash salt
½ cup quick rolled oats
　Filling (below)

Prepare desired filling (below). Set aside. Preheat oven to 375°F. In large mixing bowl cream Butter Flavor Crisco, brown sugar and vanilla until light and fluffy. Mix in flour and salt. Reserve ½ cup mixture. Press remaining mixture evenly in 13×9×2-inch pan. Bake at 375°F for 10 minutes.

In medium mixing bowl combine reserved mixture and rolled oats, mixing until crumbly. Spread desired filling evenly over baked base. Sprinkle topping mixture evenly over filling. Bake at 375°F for about 15 minutes, or until bubbly (for cream cheese filling, until set). Cool. Cut into bars, about 3×1½ inches.

Fillings:

Lime-Cream Cheese: In medium mixing bowl blend 8 ounces cream cheese, 2 tablespoons lime juice, 1 egg and ½ cup sugar until smooth. Spread over baked crust. *Pictured, top.*

Cherry: Spread 1 can (21 ounces) cherry pie filling over baked crust. *Pictured, center.*

Pineapple-Coconut: In medium saucepan combine two 8-ounce cans crushed pineapple, ½ cup sugar and 1 tablespoon cornstarch. Cook over medium heat until thickened, stirring constantly. Stir in ¼ cup chopped pecans, ½ cup flaked coconut and 1 teaspoon lemon juice. Spread over baked crust. *Pictured, bottom.*

Blueberry: Spread 1 can (21 ounces) blueberry pie filling over baked crust.

Fig: In medium saucepan combine 2 cups chopped figs (one 12-ounce package), 1 cup orange juice, ½ cup water, ½ cup sugar and dash salt. Cook over medium heat for about 10 minutes, or until mixture thickens, stirring occasionally. Spread over baked crust. **24 bars**

Orange Coconut Bars

¾ cup Butter Flavor Crisco
1 cup granulated sugar
½ cup packed brown sugar
2 eggs
⅓ cup orange juice
2 teaspoons grated orange peel
2 cups all-purpose flour
2 teaspoons baking powder
1 cup flaked coconut
Glaze:
1 cup confectioners' sugar
2 tablespoons orange juice
1 teaspoon grated orange peel

Preheat oven to 350°F. Grease 15½ × 10½ × 1-inch jelly roll pan. Set aside.

In large mixing bowl cream Butter Flavor Crisco, granulated sugar, brown sugar and eggs until light and fluffy. Blend in orange juice and peel. Mix in flour and baking powder. Stir in coconut. Spread in prepared pan. Bake at 350°F for about 20 minutes, or until light golden brown and wooden pick inserted in center comes out clean. Cool completely.

For glaze, blend confectioners' sugar, orange juice and peel. Spread glaze evenly over baked layer. Cut into bars, about 2 × 1 inch. **64 bars**

↑ Toffee Bars

⅔ cup Butter Flavor Crisco
⅔ cup packed brown sugar
1 egg
½ teaspoon vanilla
1⅓ cups all-purpose flour
¼ teaspoon salt
1⅓ cups semi-sweet chocolate chips
½ cup finely chopped nuts

Preheat oven to 350°F. Grease 13 × 9 × 2-inch pan. Set aside.

In medium mixing bowl cream Butter Flavor Crisco, brown sugar, egg and vanilla until light and fluffy. Mix in flour and salt. Spread dough evenly in prepared pan. Bake at 350°F for 15 minutes, or until golden brown. Sprinkle chocolate chips over hot crust. Return pan to oven; bake for 1 minute to melt chips. Remove from oven. Spread melted chips evenly over crust. Sprinkle nuts on top. Cool slightly. Cut into bars, about 2 × 1½ inches. Cool completely. **32 bars**

Fudgy Coconut Bars ↑

½ cup Butter Flavor Crisco
⅔ cup sugar
¼ cup cocoa
1 egg
1¼ cups all-purpose flour
¼ teaspoon salt
    Filling:
1 can (14 ounces) sweetened condensed milk
3 tablespoons all-purpose flour
1 teaspoon vanilla
⅔ cup chopped walnuts
½ cup flaked coconut
½ cup semi-sweet chocolate chips

Preheat oven to 350°F. Grease 13 × 9 × 2-inch pan. Set aside.

In medium mixing bowl blend Butter Flavor Crisco, sugar, cocoa and egg. Mix in flour and salt. Pat evenly into prepared pan. Bake for 10 to 12 minutes, or until surface is dry.

For filling, in small mixing bowl combine condensed milk, flour and vanilla. Stir in walnuts, coconut and chocolate chips. Spread onto hot crust. Bake at 350°F for 20 to 25 minutes, or until light golden brown. Cool. Cut into squares, about 1½ × 1½ inches. **48 bars**

Almond Shortbread Bars ↑

⅔ cup Butter Flavor Crisco
⅔ cup sugar
1 egg, separated
2 tablespoons milk
½ teaspoon almond extract
1½ cups all-purpose flour
1 teaspoon water
½ cup finely chopped almonds

Preheat oven to 350°F. Grease 13 × 9 × 2-inch pan. Set aside.

In medium mixing bowl cream Butter Flavor Crisco, sugar, egg yolk, milk and almond extract. Mix in flour. Press evenly in prepared pan. Add water to egg white in small mixing bowl. Beat until foamy. Brush over dough surface. Sprinkle with almonds, pressing nuts down slightly with fingertips.

Bake at 350°F for 18 to 20 minutes, or until light golden brown. Cool for 10 minutes. Cut into bars, about 2 × 1½ inches. **32 bars**

← Fried Pies

1½ cups all-purpose flour
½ cup plus 2 tablespoons sugar, divided
1 teaspoon baking powder
½ teaspoon salt
½ cup Butter Flavor Crisco
¼ to ⅓ cup milk
½ cup cherry, blueberry or lemon
  pie filling
1 teaspoon ground cinnamon
  Butter Flavor Crisco for frying

In medium mixing bowl combine flour, 2 tablespoons sugar, baking powder and salt. Cut in Butter Flavor Crisco to form coarse crumbs. Add milk, 1 tablespoon at a time, mixing with fork until particles are moistened and cling together. Form dough into ball. Divide in half. Roll each half ¼ inch thick on lightly floured board or pastry cloth. Cut into 4-inch circles. Place 2 teaspoons filling in center of each circle; fold in half. Seal edges by pressing with tines of fork. Combine remaining ½ cup sugar and cinnamon in bowl. Set aside.

In deep fat fryer or deep skillet heat 1 inch Butter Flavor Crisco to 360°F. Fry a few at a time until golden brown, turning once. Drain on paper towels. Dredge in cinnamon-sugar mixture. Serve warm.

12 individual pies

Pecan Pie

1 unbaked 9-inch pastry shell
⅓ cup Butter Flavor Crisco
⅔ cup granulated or packed brown sugar
⅔ cup light corn syrup
3 eggs, slightly beaten
1 package (6 ounces) pecan halves

Prepare pastry. Set aside.

Preheat oven to 350°F. In 1-quart saucepan melt Butter Flavor Crisco. Remove from heat. Blend in sugar, corn syrup and eggs. Stir in pecans. Pour into prepared pastry. Bake for about 50 minutes, or until set. Cool. **One 9-inch pie**

Chocolate Cream Pie →

1 baked 9-inch pastry shell
1 cup sugar
⅓ cup cornstarch
¼ teaspoon salt
2 cups milk
2 egg yolks, slightly beaten
2 squares (1 ounce each) unsweetened chocolate
1 tablespoon Butter Flavor Crisco
1 teaspoon vanilla

Prepare pastry shell. Cool. Set aside.

In 2-quart saucepan combine sugar, cornstarch and salt. Blend in milk. Cook and stir over medium heat until mixture thickens. Remove from heat. Blend small amount of hot mixture into egg yolks. Blend back into hot mixture, stirring to combine. Cook and stir over low heat until mixture boils. Boil for 1 minute, stirring constantly. Remove from heat. Add chocolate, Butter Flavor Crisco and vanilla. Stir until chocolate melts. Pour into prepared pastry shell. Refrigerate until completely cool. Serve with *whipped cream,* if desired.   **One 9-inch pie**

Graham Cracker Crust

1 cup graham cracker crumbs
¼ cup packed brown sugar
⅓ cup Butter Flavor Crisco, melted

Preheat oven to 350°F.

In small mixing bowl combine graham cracker crumbs and brown sugar. Mix well. Stir in melted Butter Flavor Crisco. Press into 9-inch pie plate. Bake at 350°F for 10 minutes. Cool completely before filling.

Chocolate Crumb Crust: Follow the recipe above, substituting 1⅓ cups crushed chocolate wafers for the brown sugar and graham cracker crumbs.
          One 9-inch crust

Sour Cream Pastry ↑

1 cup all-purpose flour
1 tablespoon sugar
¼ teaspoon salt
⅓ cup Butter Flavor Crisco
3 tablespoons dairy sour cream

Preheat oven to 350°F.

In medium mixing bowl combine flour, sugar and salt. Cut in Butter Flavor Crisco to form coarse crumbs. Add sour cream, mixing with fork until particles are moistened and cling together. Form dough into ball. Roll on lightly floured board or pastry cloth to a circle at least 2 inches larger than inverted 9-inch pie plate. Fit into pie plate. Trim and flute. Bake at 350°F for 10 to 12 minutes, or until lightly browned.   **One 9-inch pastry shell**

Banana Cream Pie

1 baked 9-inch pastry shell
²⁄₃ cup sugar
¼ cup cornstarch
¼ teaspoon salt
2 cups milk
2 egg yolks, slightly beaten
1 tablespoon Butter Flavor Crisco
1½ teaspoons vanilla
1 large banana

Prepare pastry shell. Cool. Set aside.

In 2-quart saucepan combine sugar, cornstarch and salt. Blend in milk. Cook and stir over medium heat until mixture thickens. Remove from heat. Blend small amount of hot mixture into egg yolks. Blend back into hot mixture, stirring to combine. Cook and stir over medium heat until mixture boils. Boil for about 1 minute, stirring constantly. Remove from heat. Blend in Butter Flavor Crisco and vanilla. Cool to lukewarm.

Thinly slice banana; arrange slices evenly on bottom and sides of pastry shell. Pour filling over bananas, spreading evenly. Refrigerate until completely cool. Top with *whipped cream*, if desired.

Coconut Cream Pie: Follow the recipe above, omitting banana. Stir ²⁄₃ cup flaked coconut into filling after adding Butter Flavor Crisco and vanilla.

One 9-inch pie

↑Applesauce Pie

1 unbaked 9-inch Sour Cream Pastry shell
¾ cup sugar
¼ cup all-purpose flour
½ teaspoon salt
¼ teaspoon ground cinnamon
1 jar (15 ounces) applesauce (1½ cups)
¼ cup Butter Flavor Crisco
3 eggs

Preheat oven to 425°F. Prepare Sour Cream Pastry as directed, page 145, but do not bake.

In medium mixing bowl combine sugar, flour, salt, cinnamon, applesauce, Butter Flavor Crisco and eggs. Blend thoroughly with wire whisk. Pour into prepared pastry. Bake at 425°F for 10 minutes. Reduce oven temperature to 350°F. Bake for 20 to 30 minutes longer, or until center is set. Cool completely. Top with *whipped cream*, if desired.

One 9-inch pie

Crêpes With Orange Sauce ↑

    1   recipe Crêpes
    ¼   cup Butter Flavor Crisco
    ½   cup packed brown sugar
    ¼   cup orange juice
    1   tablespoon grated orange peel
    1   tablespoon brandy or apple juice
        Confectioners' sugar

Prepare dessert-size Crêpes as directed, page 109.

In 1-quart saucepan blend Butter Flavor Crisco and brown sugar. Add orange juice and peel. Cook and stir over low heat until mixture boils. Boil for 1 minute, stirring constantly. Pour into medium skillet. Blend in brandy. Place over very low heat. Add crêpes one at a time. Coat both sides. Fold in half and in half again. Stack off to side of pan. Repeat with remaining crêpes. Sift confectioners' sugar over crêpes. Serve warm. **6 to 8 servings**

Easy Fruit Cobbler

    1   package (9 ounce) yellow cake mix
    1   can (21 ounce) cherry, blueberry or
        peach pie filling
    ¼   cup Butter Flavor Crisco, melted

Preheat oven to 350°F. Lightly grease 1½ quart casserole.

In prepared casserole layer half the pie filling and half the dry cake mix. Repeat layers.

Pour melted Butter Flavor Crisco evenly over top layer. Bake at 350°F for 60 to 65 minutes, or until light golden brown. Serve with *vanilla ice cream*, if desired. **4 to 6 servings**

Lemon Cream Cheese Dessert Roll →

Cake:
3 eggs
¾ cup sugar
½ teaspoon vanilla
¾ cup all-purpose flour
1 teaspoon baking powder
⅛ teaspoon salt

Lemon Layer:
½ cup sugar
2 tablespoons plus 1 teaspoon cornstarch
⅛ teaspoon salt
½ cup water
3 tablespoons lemon juice
1 teaspoon grated lemon peel
1 egg yolk, beaten
2 tablespoons Butter Flavor Crisco

Cream Cheese Layer:
1 package (3 ounces) cream cheese, softened
1 tablespoon Butter Flavor Crisco
1 teaspoon lemon juice
½ cup confectioners' sugar
1 teaspoon milk
Confectioners' sugar

Preheat oven to 375°F. Line 15½ × 10½ × 1-inch jelly roll pan with wax paper; grease. Set aside.

For cake, in large mixing bowl beat eggs at medium speed of electric mixer for about 5 minutes, or until foamy and lemon colored. Gradually beat in sugar. Blend in vanilla. Add flour, baking powder and salt. Beat at low speed until just blended. Pour into prepared pan. Bake at 375°F for 8 to 10 minutes, or until wooden pick inserted in center comes out clean. Loosen warm cake from edges of pan. Invert onto towel dusted generously with confectioners' sugar. Trim crisp edges if necessary. Roll cake in towel, starting at narrow end. Cool completely.

For lemon layer, in small saucepan combine sugar, cornstarch and salt. Blend in water, lemon juice and peel. Cook over medium heat until thick and translucent, stirring constantly. Remove from heat. Blend small amount of hot mixture into egg yolk. Blend back into hot mixture, stirring to combine. Stir in Butter Flavor Crisco until smooth. Cool completely, stirring occasionally.

For cream cheese layer, in small bowl blend cream cheese, Butter Flavor Crisco and lemon juice. Mix in confectioners' sugar. Blend in milk. Set aside. Continue as directed below.   **6 to 8 servings**

How to Assemble Dessert Roll

Unroll cooled cake; remove towel. Spread cream cheese mixture, then the cooled lemon mixture evenly over cake.

Reroll cake tightly. Place seam side down on serving plate.

Sift confectioners' sugar over cake. Cover and refrigerate until lemon filling is set.

Apple Maple Steamed Pudding

¼ cup Butter Flavor Crisco
½ cup packed brown sugar
1 egg
⅓ cup maple syrup
1¾ cups all-purpose flour
1 teaspoon baking powder
1 teaspoon ground cinnamon
½ teaspoon baking soda
½ teaspoon ground ginger
½ cup buttermilk
1 cup chopped apples
Hard Sauce

Grease ovenproof 6-cup mold or pudding basin. Dust with granulated sugar. Set aside. In medium mixing bowl combine Butter Flavor Crisco, brown sugar, egg and maple syrup. Beat at low speed of electric mixer until blended. Add flour, baking powder, cinnamon, baking soda, ginger and buttermilk. Beat at medium speed until blended, scraping bowl frequently. Stir in apples. Spoon into mold. Cover mold tightly with double thickness of heavy-duty foil.

Place 1 inch water in Dutch oven. Place filled mold on rack in Dutch oven. Cover. Cook over high heat until water boils. Reduce heat. Cook at very slow boil over low heat for 2 to 2½ hours, or until wooden pick inserted in center of pudding comes out clean. (If necessary to add water during steaming, lift lid and quickly add boiling water.) Remove mold from Dutch oven. Remove foil. Allow steam to escape before unmolding. Serve with Hard Sauce, page 155.   **6 to 8 servings**

✝Bananas Royale

⅓ cup packed brown sugar
¼ cup Butter Flavor Crisco
¼ cup half-and-half
½ teaspoon ground cinnamon
¼ teaspoon ground nutmeg
3 large bananas, peeled and sliced
3 tablespoons brandy, optional
Vanilla ice cream

In medium skillet combine brown sugar, Butter Flavor Crisco, half-and-half, cinnamon and nutmeg. Cook and stir over medium heat until mixture boils. Boil and stir for 2 minutes. Remove from heat. Add sliced bananas, stirring gently to coat. Cook over low heat for about 2 minutes, or until soft, stirring occasionally. Stir in brandy. Serve over ice cream.   **4 to 6 servings**

Peach Refrigerator Squares

⅔ cup Butter Flavor Crisco
2 cups graham cracker crumbs
⅓ cup sugar
1 quart vanilla ice cream, softened
1 package (3¾ ounces) instant lemon
   pudding mix
1 cup milk
1 can (16 ounces) sliced peaches, drained
   and chopped

Preheat oven to 350°F. In 1-quart saucepan melt Butter Flavor Crisco. Remove from heat. Stir in graham cracker crumbs and sugar. Reserve 2 tablespoons for top. Press remaining crumbs into bottom of 13 × 9-inch pan. Bake at 350°F for 10 minutes. Cool on wire rack.

In large mixing bowl combine softened ice cream, pudding mix and milk. Beat at low speed of electric mixer until blended. Fold in peaches. Spread over cooled crust. Sprinkle with reserved crumbs. Refrigerate for at least 2 hours, or until set. Cut into 12 pieces. **12 servings**

Chocolate Mint Parfait Squares ✝

Crust:
⅓ cup Butter Flavor Crisco, melted
1⅓ cups crushed chocolate wafers
Filling:
¾ cup Butter Flavor Crisco
1½ cups confectioners' sugar
3 squares (1 ounce each) unsweetened
   chocolate, melted
3 eggs
1 teaspoon peppermint extract
1 teaspoon vanilla
Topping:
2 cups prepared whipped topping
½ cup chopped maraschino cherries,
   drained

Preheat oven to 350°F.

For crust, combine melted Butter Flavor Crisco and crushed wafers. Press into 10 × 6-inch baking dish. Bake at 350°F for 5 minutes. Cool on wire rack.

For filling, in medium mixing bowl cream Butter Flavor Crisco and confectioners' sugar. Blend in melted chocolate. Add eggs, peppermint extract and vanilla. Beat at medium speed of electric mixer until blended. Spread evenly over cooled crust. Set aside.

For topping, in small mixing bowl combine whipped topping and cherries. Spread evenly over chocolate layer. Freeze for at least 2 hours, or until firm. Cut into 8 pieces. Garnish with *shaved chocolate*, if desired. **8 servings**

151

Cherry Cream Cheese Dessert Strudels →

Filling:

2 packages (3 ounces each) cream cheese, softened
2 tablespoons Butter Flavor Crisco
1 egg, separated
½ cup sugar
2 tablespoons all-purpose flour
½ teaspoon almond extract
½ cup chopped maraschino cherries, drained

Dough:

2 cups all-purpose flour
1 teaspoon sugar
¼ teaspoon salt
¾ cup Butter Flavor Crisco
4 to 5 tablespoons cold water

Glaze:

1 cup confectioners' sugar
¼ teaspoon almond extract
4 to 5 teaspoons milk
2 tablespoons sliced almonds

Preheat oven to 350°F. Grease baking sheet. Set aside.

For filling, in medium mixing bowl combine cream cheese, Butter Flavor Crisco, egg yolk, sugar, flour and almond extract. Beat at medium speed of electric mixer until smooth and fluffy. Stir in cherries. Set aside.

For dough, in medium mixing bowl combine flour, sugar and salt. Cut in Butter Flavor Crisco to form coarse crumbs. Add water, 1 tablespoon at a time, mixing with fork until particles are moistened and cling together. Form dough into ball. Divide in half. Continue as directed under photos below.

For glaze, in small mixing bowl combine confectioners' sugar, almond extract and enough milk to make smooth glaze. Drizzle over tops of strudels. Sprinkle each with 1 tablespoon almonds.

Two 12-inch dessert pastries

How to Assemble Dessert Strudels

Flatten one ball into rectangular shape. Roll into a 14 × 9-inch rectangle on lightly floured board.

Spread ¾ cup filling over half of dough, beginning slightly off center and spreading to within 1 inch of edges to form a 12 × 3-inch rectangle.

Fold ends and sides of dough over filling. Moisten edges with water. Fold upper half of dough over and seal edges.

Place seam side down on one side of prepared baking sheet. Repeat for remaining dough and filling.

Prick each strudel several times with tines of fork. Beat egg white until foamy.

Brush on tops of strudels. Bake at 350°F for 40 to 45 minutes, or until golden brown. Cool slightly. Glaze as directed above.

Butter Rum Sauce ↟

  1 cup packed brown sugar
 ⅓ cup Butter Flavor Crisco
 ½ cup dark corn syrup
 ¼ cup milk
  1 teaspoon rum flavoring

In 1-quart saucepan blend brown sugar, Butter Flavor Crisco and corn syrup. Cook and stir over low heat until sugar dissolves; do not boil. Remove from heat. Gradually blend in milk until smooth. Stir in rum flavoring. Serve warm. **1¾ cups sauce**

Hot Fudge Topping ↟

  1 cup sugar
  1 can (5⅓ ounces) evaporated milk
  1 tablespoon light corn syrup
  2 squares (1 ounce each) unsweetened
      chocolate or semisweet chocolate
      (for sweeter sauce)
  3 tablespoons Butter Flavor Crisco
  1 teaspoon vanilla
 ¼ teaspoon salt

In 2-quart saucepan combine sugar, evaporated milk and corn syrup. Heat to full rolling boil, stirring constantly. Boil for 1 minute, stirring constantly. Reduce heat. Add chocolate. Stir over low heat to melt completely. Remove from heat. Blend in Butter Flavor Crisco, vanilla and salt. Serve warm.

1½ cups topping

Peanut Butter Sauce

- ½ cup packed brown sugar
- ⅓ cup light corn syrup
- ¼ cup Butter Flavor Crisco
- ½ cup peanut butter
- ¼ cup milk
- ½ teaspoon vanilla

In 1-quart saucepan blend brown sugar, corn syrup and Butter Flavor Crisco. Cook and stir over low heat until mixture just comes to a boil. Remove from heat. Blend in peanut butter until melted. Gradually blend in milk until mixture is smooth. Cook and stir over low heat until mixture returns to a boil. Remove from heat. Stir in vanilla. Serve warm. **1½ cups sauce**

Hard Sauce †

- ¼ cup Butter Flavor Crisco
- 2 tablespoons brandy or apple juice
- 1½ cups confectioners' sugar
  Dash ground nutmeg

In small mixing bowl combine Butter Flavor Crisco and brandy. Beat at low speed of electric mixer for 1 minute. Add confectioners' sugar and nutmeg. Beat at medium speed until smooth. Spoon into small bowl or mold. Refrigerate for at least 1 hour, or until firm. **1 cup sauce**

CANDIES

← Raisin Nut Clusters

    8 ounces chocolate confectioners' coating
    2 tablespoons Butter Flavor Crisco
1½ cups broken walnuts
    ½ cup raisins

Line baking sheet with wax paper. Set aside.

In double boiler or 2-quart saucepan over very low heat, melt confectioners' coating and Butter Flavor Crisco, stirring constantly. Remove from heat. Add walnuts and raisins. Mix well to coat. Drop by heaping tablespoonfuls onto prepared baking sheet. Refrigerate for at least 30 minutes, or until set.

1½ to 2 dozen candies

← Pralines

1½ cups packed brown sugar
    1 cup granulated sugar
    1 can (5⅓ ounces) evaporated milk
    1 tablespoon light corn syrup
    3 tablespoons Butter Flavor Crisco
    ½ teaspoon vanilla
1½ cups coarsely chopped pecans
    ¼ teaspoon cream of tartar

Lightly grease baking sheet (line with greased foil, if desired). Set aside.

In 3-quart saucepan combine brown sugar, granulated sugar, evaporated milk and corn syrup. Heat to boiling over medium heat, stirring constantly. Cover and boil for 1 minute. Uncover. Insert candy thermometer. Cook over medium heat, without stirring, to 235°F. Remove from heat.

Add Butter Flavor Crisco, vanilla, pecans and cream of tartar. Stir with wooden spoon until mixture thickens slightly. Do not overstir. Quickly drop by rounded tablespoonfuls onto prepared baking sheet. Cool until firm. **About 3 dozen candies**

Peanut Brittle ↑

1½ cups sugar
¾ cup light corn syrup
½ teaspoon salt
1½ cups raw peanuts
1 tablespoon Butter Flavor Crisco
1½ teaspoons vanilla
1½ teaspoons baking soda

Grease 15½ × 12-inch baking sheet. Set aside.

In 3-quart saucepan combine sugar, corn syrup, salt and peanuts. Cook and stir over medium-low heat to 240°F on candy thermometer. Add Butter Flavor Crisco and vanilla. Continue to cook and stir until 300°F. Stir in baking soda. Immediately pour onto prepared baking sheet and spread quickly into even layer, about ¼ inch thick. Cool completely. Break into pieces.   **1½ pounds candy**

Truffles ↑

8 squares (1 ounce each) semi-sweet chocolate
⅓ cup half-and-half
⅓ cup Butter Flavor Crisco
3 egg yolks
⅓ cup confectioners' sugar
2 tablespoons dark rum or half-and-half
⅔ cup finely chopped nuts

In 1½-quart saucepan combine chocolate and half-and-half. Cook and stir over low heat until chocolate melts and mixture is smooth. Remove from heat. Add Butter Flavor Crisco, stirring until melted.

Add egg yolks, confectioners' sugar and rum. Beat at medium speed of electric mixer until blended. Refrigerate for about 2 hours, or until firm.

Shape mixture into 1-inch balls. Roll each ball in nuts to coat. Chill in refrigerator.
                    About 2½ dozen candies

Fudge

2 cups sugar
1 can (5⅓ ounces) evaporated milk
1 tablespoon light corn syrup
2 squares (1 ounce each)
   unsweetened chocolate
½ teaspoon salt
2 tablespoons Butter Flavor Crisco
1 teaspoon vanilla
½ cup chopped nuts, optional

Lightly grease 8×8×2-inch pan. Set aside.

In 3-quart saucepan combine sugar, evaporated milk, corn syrup, chocolate and salt. Heat to boiling over medium heat, stirring constantly. Cover and boil for 1 minute. Uncover. Insert candy thermometer. Cook over medium heat, without stirring, to 236°F. Remove from heat.

Add Butter Flavor Crisco and do not stir. Cool undisturbed to 120°F. Add vanilla. Beat vigorously until mixture starts to thicken and lose its sheen. Quickly stir in nuts. Spread in prepared pan. Cool until firm. Cut into 1-inch squares.

Peanut Butter Fudge: Follow the recipe above, substituting 1 cup brown sugar and 1 cup granulated sugar for the granulated sugar. Omit chocolate. Add ¼ cup peanut butter with Butter Flavor Crisco. Omit vanilla.   **About 1 pound candy**

✝ Sugared Pecan Halves

1½ cups sugar
½ cup orange juice
2 tablespoons Butter Flavor Crisco
2 tablespoons light corn syrup
½ teaspoon ground cinnamon
¼ teaspoon ground cloves
2 packages (6 ounces each) pecan
   halves (4 cups)

In 2-quart saucepan combine sugar, orange juice, Butter Flavor Crisco, corn syrup, cinnamon and cloves. Cook over medium heat, stirring constantly, to 240°F on candy thermometer. Stir in pecans. Pour onto greased baking sheet, spreading into thin layer. Cool completely. Break to separate nuts.

About 4 cups candy

Chocolate Peanut Butter Bites ➔

½ cup peanut butter
4 tablespoons Butter Flavor Crisco, divided
¾ cup graham cracker crumbs
¼ cup confectioners' sugar
1 package (5¾ ounces) milk chocolate chips

Line 9-inch pie plate with foil. Set aside.

In medium mixing bowl combine peanut butter, 2 tablespoons Butter Flavor Crisco, graham cracker crumbs and confectioners' sugar. Mix well. (Mixture will be stiff.) Set aside.

In double boiler or small saucepan over very low heat, melt chocolate chips and remaining 2 tablespoons Butter Flavor Crisco, stirring constantly. Remove from heat.

Pour half the melted chocolate mixture into prepared pie plate. Spread chocolate about ½ inch up sides of pie plate. Place in freezer for about 10 minutes, or until set.

Remove from freezer. Spread peanut butter mixture over set chocolate. Pour remaining melted chocolate over peanut butter layer, spreading to edges. Place in freezer or refrigerator to set. Cut or break into bite-size pieces.   **1 pound candy**

Caramels

1 cup sugar
½ cup Butter Flavor Crisco
1 teaspoon vanilla
1 cup dark corn syrup
¾ cup milk
1 cup chopped pecans or walnuts, optional

Line bottom and sides of 9×9×2-inch pan with foil. Grease foil. Set aside.

In 3-quart saucepan blend sugar, Butter Flavor Crisco and vanilla. Stir in corn syrup and milk. Cook over medium heat, stirring constantly, to 246°F on candy thermometer. Stir in nuts. Pour into prepared pan. Let stand until firm and completely cool. Cut into 1-inch squares.
1½ pounds candy

Chocolate Mints ↑

1 egg
½ teaspoon mint extract
1 package (6 ounces) semi-sweet
  chocolate chips (1 cup)
2 tablespoons Butter Flavor Crisco

Line baking sheet with wax paper. Set aside.

In small bowl beat together egg and mint extract.
Set aside.

In double boiler or small saucepan over very low
heat, melt chocolate chips and Butter Flavor Crisco,
stirring constantly. Gradually add to egg mixture,
beating until smooth. Drop by rounded teaspoonfuls
onto prepared baking sheet. Refrigerate for about 2
hours, or until firm.

2½ to 3 dozen candies

Cream Cheese Mints ↑

1 package (3 ounces) cream cheese,
  softened
¼ cup Butter Flavor Crisco
½ teaspoon mint extract
3 to 3½ cups confectioners' sugar
1 to 3 drops food coloring, any color

Line baking sheet with wax paper. Set aside.

In medium mixing bowl blend cream cheese, Butter
Flavor Crisco and mint extract. Beat in
confectioners' sugar at low speed of electric mixer
until mixture is very stiff and crumbly. Add food
coloring. (To make mints different colors, divide
mixture and tint each part.)

Shape by ½-teaspoonfuls into balls. Place on
prepared baking sheet. Using fork tines dipped in
confectioners' sugar, flatten each candy in crisscross
pattern to ¼ inch thick. Or, if desired, shape using
mint molds. Let stand overnight to dry.

8 to 9 dozen candies

Peanut Butter Nut Roll ➺

3 tablespoons light corn syrup
2 tablespoons Butter Flavor Crisco
2 tablespoons half-and-half
1 package (11½ ounces) peanut butter chips (2 cups)
1 teaspoon vanilla
1 cup chopped salted peanuts, optional

Filling:
2 tablespoons Butter Flavor Crisco
3 cups miniature marshmallows
1 tablespoon half-and-half

Line baking sheet with wax paper; grease. Set aside. In small saucepan combine corn syrup, Butter Flavor Crisco, half-and-half, peanut butter chips and vanilla. Cook over low heat, stirring constantly, until mixture is smooth. Stir in peanuts. Continue as directed below.

About 3 dozen candies

How to Assemble Peanut Butter Nut Roll

Spread mixture into a 17 × 8-inch rectangle on prepared wax paper. Set aside. For filling, in small saucepan melt Butter Flavor Crisco over low heat.

Stir in marshmallows and half-and-half. Continue to cook and stir over low heat until marshmallows melt and mixture is smooth. Remove from heat.

Spread filling to within 1 inch of edges of peanut butter layer. Beginning with longest edge, roll into log. Refrigerate for about 1 hour, or until firm. Cut into ½-inch slices.

161

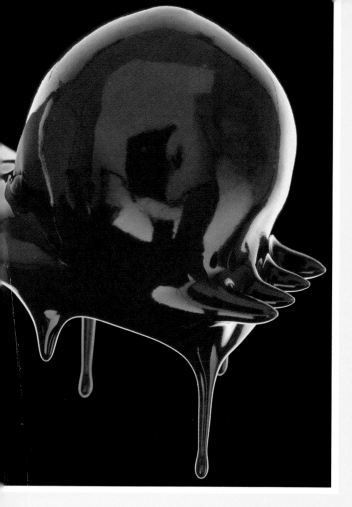

Granola Chews

⅓ cup Butter Flavor Crisco
½ cup packed brown sugar
¼ cup honey
2 tablespoons maple syrup
1½ cups rolled oats
½ cup raisins
½ cup chopped dried apples or apricots
½ cup chopped walnuts
½ cup flaked coconut
1 teaspoon vanilla
½ teaspoon ground cinnamon
¼ teaspoon salt
⅓ cup confectioners' sugar

In 1½-quart saucepan combine Butter Flavor Crisco, brown sugar, honey and maple syrup. Heat to boiling over low heat, stirring constantly. Boil and stir 1 minute. Set aside.

In large mixing bowl combine rolled oats, raisins, apples, walnuts, coconut, vanilla, cinnamon and salt. Add brown sugar mixture. Mix well. Cool. Shape by rounded teaspoonfuls into balls. Roll in confectioners' sugar. Store in refrigerator.

About 3 dozen candies

↑ Chocolate Orange Candy

1½ cups graham cracker crumbs
1 cup confectioners' sugar
1 cup flaked coconut
¼ cup Butter Flavor Crisco
¼ cup frozen orange juice concentrate
2 tablespoons light corn syrup
Coating:
1½ cups semi-sweet chocolate chips
1 tablespoon plus 2 teaspoons Butter Flavor Crisco

In medium mixing bowl combine graham cracker crumbs, confectioners' sugar, coconut, Butter Flavor Crisco, orange juice concentrate and corn syrup. Beat at low speed of electric mixer until blended. (Mixture will be crumbly.) Shape into 1-inch balls. Place on tray and freeze for 30 minutes.

Line baking-sheet with waxed paper. Set aside.

For coating, in double boiler or small saucepan over very low heat, melt chocolate chips and Butter Flavor Crisco, stirring constantly. Remove from heat. Dip each ball in chocolate mixture to coat. Place on prepared baking sheet to set. Store in refrigerator. **4½ to 5 dozen candies**

Penuche →

1½ cups packed brown sugar
½ cup half-and-half
   Dash salt
2 tablespoons Butter Flavor Crisco
¾ teaspoon vanilla
⅓ cup chopped pecans

Lightly grease an 8 × 4 × 2-inch loaf pan. Set aside.

In 2-quart saucepan combine brown sugar, half-and-half and salt. Heat to boiling over medium heat, stirring constantly. Cover and boil for 1 minute. Uncover. Insert candy thermometer. Cook over medium heat, without stirring, to 236°F. Remove from heat.

Add Butter Flavor Crisco and do not stir. Cool undisturbed to 120°F. Add vanilla. Beat vigorously until mixture starts to thicken and lose its sheen. Stir in pecans. Spread in prepared pan. Cut into 1-inch squares. Cool until firm.

Mexican Orange Candy: Follow the recipe above, adding 1 tablespoon grated orange rind with Butter Flavor Crisco.   **32 candies**

Chocolate-Covered Nut Creams ↑

1 can (14 ounces) sweetened
   condensed milk
¾ cup Butter Flavor Crisco
2 teaspoons vanilla
   Dash salt
1 cup finely chopped nuts
8 to 9 cups confectioners' sugar
   Coating:
3 cups semi-sweet chocolate chips
6 tablespoons Butter Flavor Crisco

Lightly grease 8 × 8 × 2- or 9 × 9 × 2-inch pan. Set aside.

In large mixing bowl blend sweetened condensed milk, Butter Flavor Crisco, vanilla and salt. Stir in nuts. Blend in confectioners' sugar until mixture is very stiff.

Press into prepared pan. Chill thoroughly. Cut into 64 squares. Remove pieces from pan. Set aside.

Line baking sheet with wax paper. Set aside.

For coating, in double boiler or small saucepan over very low heat, melt chocolate chips and Butter Flavor Crisco, stirring constantly. Remove from heat. Dip candies in chocolate mixture to coat. Place on prepared baking sheet. Let stand until set.

64 candies

Index

165